The Essential 4-Step System for Leaders to Encourage Top Teamwork at Their Workplace

Improve Your Leadership Communication, Team Building and Employee Management Skills

2nd edition

Oscar Stone

TABLE OF CONTENTS

The Most Critical Core Values of a Successful Team

(Never lead a team without these 7 values.)

7 CORE VALUES OF A
SUCCESSFUL TEAM

<u>Why is it important to set team values?</u>

Values define what your company cares about. They represent the goals and intentions of an organisation, and tell employees how their work spirit should look like. If the wrong values are set, overall productivity and work relationships will get damaged.

To receive your Team Values List for **free**, visit this link:

https://starkingbooks.activehosted.com/f/1

Introduction

Coming together is a beginning, staying together is progress, and working together is success.
—HENRY FORD

There's a lot going on within team dynamics. Nowadays, teams consist of a wide range of talent, from employees who work on-premise to employees who work remotely. Thanks to the technology sandstorm of the 20th century, members of the same organisation could even be working in a different country or continent. So, how do you make sure that your team remains motivated at work and that the company runs like a well-oiled machine? How do you cultivate an atmosphere of positive energy at the workplace where employees can come in every day feeling excited and inspired to give their best effort? By encouraging *great teamwork*.

You see, teamwork is the essence of all organisations, big or small. The group of people who unite to achieve a common goal will be the deciding factor as to whether a business succeeds or not. Members of the team must work together effectively with one aim in mind: to increase performance and productivity, or the company isn't going to survive for very long. But how does such a top team come about?

Employees spend most of their time, several hours a day, five days a week, at work. A positive, comfortable work environment is crucial to overall motivation and therefore, success. At the workplace, all members should work together instead of against one another. A motivated team embraces challenges and enjoys problem-solving because they know they have the opportunity to combine different solutions, talents, and abilities into one big productive final solution. In an ideal team scenario, new ideas flourish, and goals are achieved much faster thanks to the varied group of skillsets present.

Is creating such a team dynamic possible? *Absolutely,* especially when a smart leader is sitting at the head of the team. He or she is the person who's responsible for overseeing all of this. Every team needs someone who leads and guides the group. Whether you're in the position of a boss or simply a member of the team with a natural inclination to take charge of situations, leaders make sure that the unit holds together and becomes the highest calibre team possible.

People are capable of extraordinary accomplishments, but they rarely ever achieve this on their own. Behind every success story are the people who have had a hand in shaping that story, each with a role to play. Some of the greatest achievements in history have been the end result of the *greatness of many*. It was never about one person doing it all. It was about a team of people who came together beautifully, to create a legacy of success that lives on for years to come. That's the power of great leadership and teamwork.

Everything that you *need* to become an awesome *leader* and to harness the *power of teamwork* is within the next few chapters. Achieving a great team dynamic is not as difficult as it seems, despite the diversity and different personalities involved, and it all starts with the decision to stop managing and *start leading* effectively.

In leadership, a wealth of knowledge is waiting to be used. With the right tools and strategies at hand, everyone is able to make better teamwork happen. I certainly was lacking these strategies and tools at the beginning of my career. But after many years of trial and error, I started to understand team dynamics and how to lead people successfully. Learning from my mistakes and experiences brought me to where I am now, and I'm grateful for all the ups and downs throughout my journey. There's a lot of value and wisdom to be gained from experience, and that's why I decided to write this book.

I have been working with start-ups and big businesses alike for close to two decades now. In this time, I have picked up some management tactics—what works and what doesn't. More so than anything else, I learned that people just want to feel validated; they want to feel worth it. It's very similar to the relationship I have with my daughter or my wife. At the end of the day, we are all just human beings, and we want to relate to each other as equals. I've noticed an increasing rise in this trend with the generational shift within the workforce. And, that's the reason why new leaders must evolve with time.

After spending the past six years working for a top-notch marketing agency in the UK where I managed five different generations of workers at once, I felt compelled to share my valuable insight. The 4-step system you're going to learn is the result of my experience that I've accumulated in different leadership positions. I hope this book will help you bypass the mistakes I've made and assist you to step boldly into your role as a team leader.

Step I:
Evolving Into an Effective Leader

CHAPTER 1:

Where Does Teamwork Start?

None of us is as smart as all of us. —KEN BLANCHARD

*E*veryone can make a difference; every person can encourage top teamwork. But before we can become the source of a thriving team, we first need to understand the concept of teamwork and leadership. Think of teamwork as a fruit tree; the beautiful treetop is based on a firmly rooted trunk. Without that trunk, the branches wouldn't be able to hold together, and the whole tree would fall apart. But if the trunk stands its ground and makes sure that the leaves and flowers get enough water, it enables the tree to bear fruit as a unit. The same goes for teamwork. Only if a strong leader supports and fuels the whole team will they achieve the desired results. Every person can become the trunk of a tree. Everyone can evolve into an effective leader; and that's exactly where great teamwork starts.

John C. Maxwell, American speaker and author, once said: *"A leader is someone who knows the way, goes the way and shows everyone else the way."* Leadership is something that cannot be forced. If you do, you will fail every time. The problem is, the real message of what it means to be a great leader has been lost over the years.

What Is Leadership?

Sun Tzu, the author of *The Art of War,* believed that a leader works best when people barely know he exists. When a great leader is present, the job fulfilled, and the goal accomplished, the people believe *"we did it ourselves."* (Coming back to the tree example, actually, the branches are the ones who are bearing and holding the fruits, but it's the trunk that makes it possible in the first place.) He wrote:

"The General who advances without coveting fame and retreats without fearing disgrace, whose only thought is to protect the country and do service for his sovereign, is the jewel of the Kingdom."

The Art of War is among the many must-read books recommended by top leaders today for a reason. Another example of an excellent leadership theory was put forth by the Roman consul in the first century, Cicero. He believed that a leader can only deliver results if he does it through other people. According to Cicero, the leader has to focus his attention on others if he wants anything to happen or change. All of these wise scholars and philosophers believed that leadership was not about dominion but about service.

On the other hand, in the 16th century, Niccolo Machiavelli wrote *The Prince,* in which he stated that everything was "all about the leader." Machiavelli believed that the leader must maintain power at all costs, and the focus must be entirely upon him. He had to retain control by force or deceit, if need be. Machiavelli's approach is both confusing and contradictory to what good leadership should be, and unfortunately, we are still clearing up his misconception of leadership today. The same goes for Scott Thomas Carlyle (British Historian), who believed that leaders were born and not made. You either had the makings of a great leader, or you did not. If you had it, then you had the power to achieve greatness. If you did not? Well, that was too bad for you. You were either a leader or a follower, according to Carlyle. These beliefs have lingered on today like a bad smell that won't go away, and they have muddied the waters of what effective leadership looks like. I hope you haven't been affected by this plague. Nevertheless, let's clear our views on leadership once and for all.

The best leaders don't create more followers,
they create more leaders. —Tom Peters

Leadership is actually very simple. It's not easy, but it is simple. It is more about *who you are than what you do*, and it comes down to a few elementary rules. If you're able to grasp these rules and put them into practice, it's going to be impossible *not to inspire* others. A leader can effectively manage their team and bring out the best in everyone under their guidance. But great leadership can be nerve-wracking. Being an effective leader to a group of people who are counting on you to encourage them and steer them in the right direction is a lot of responsibility.

So, what makes an effective leader? As I've learned throughout the path of my career, it is a cumulation of several things, to be honest. Let's start with the number one principle of leadership: It is not about you. Every step you take as a leader moving forward starts from this one principle. Like Eleanor Roosevelt once said:

"A good leader can inspire people to have confidence in the leader. A great leader can inspire people to have confidence in themselves."

Every leader is only a leader when they have followers. But the best leaders don't create more followers. They create more great leaders. They realise that they are not the hero of the day who swoops in and solves all the problems and answers all the questions. The world is too complex for just one person to have all the answers. And yet, a lot of people still believe that is what leaders are supposed to do.

All successful leaders have a healthy mix of several qualities that contribute to their overall success, they:

- Improve the traits they are lacking
- Always educate themselves
- Believe in their abilities
- Focus on doing things of greater value
- Hold themselves accountable
- Are great contributors
- Are able to handle pressure
- Demonstrate mutual respect
- Are role models

The hardest journey is identifying what qualities you'll have to cultivate and learn. Which one of these do you need to improve on? And how do you want to do it? There's a note section at the end of the book to write down your ideas and thoughts. By taking notes, you can more actively engage with the content, which will help you better remember what you've read. I know it feels nerdy, but don't let that stop you from making the best of this book *and* your time. Let's take a look at each of these characteristics.

Leaders Improve the Traits They Are Lacking

Great leaders are not afraid to admit they have weaknesses. They never stop developing, and they have the willpower to prevent themselves from getting stuck and too cosy in their comfort zone (the biggest danger area of success). But only when you know where improvement is needed can you work on making it better. If a quality is missing, work on it until you've mastered it—master one quality before moving onto the next.

Leaders Always Educate Themselves

Never be satisfied. The key trait in building the leadership qualities that will propel you to success is to continually learn by taking courses, reading books, watching TED Talks and listening to podcasts. Always read and always study. No matter how busy they are, the best leaders are those that never stop learning. The *average CEO reads 52 books* in a year. That's one book every week! Most people struggle to finish one book a month, let alone a week. As the 6th President of the United States, John Quincy Adams once said:

"You're a leader if your actions inspire others to learn more, dream more, become more and do more."

Leaders never stop learning, and they never compromise on reading. I have trouble with this myself. It is hard to find time for reading, especially on a busy day. Therefore, I made it a habit to read at least 15 minutes every evening before going to bed. If you picked up this book, it means you're heading in the right direction, so keep it up and never ever stop. There is always room for more knowledge.

Leaders Believe in Their Abilities

The most successful people don't worry about what happened in the past or the mistakes they made. The future is what matters. If you have never been a leader before, it doesn't mean that you can't become one in the future. But before you can lead others, you need to be confident enough in your own ability to do so. Other people will not follow your leadership and commands if you are not sure about the decisions you make yourself. No one is going to believe in a leader who is regularly nervous and second-guessing their own decisions.

An effective leader needs always to display both *confidence and assertiveness*, a strength that others can take comfort in. You don't have to be overconfident, but you do need to reflect a certain degree of confidence, which allows your followers to develop trust in you as a leader. Leaders know what they want and then set out to make it happen.

Leaders Focus on Doing Things of Greater Value

All great leaders focus on the things that are going to add value and deliver results. Read more, listen more, exercise more patience, whatever it takes. While you're doing that, you'll need to deliberately spend less time on activities that impede your success or that don't help you move ahead faster. *Focus on doing what you do for the future.* It's time to take a step back and look at your current priorities and strategies. What's working, and what is only a distraction? For example, is watching TV bringing you closer to your goal? If something isn't working and hasn't been for a while, it's time to rethink it and stop wasting any more time on it. This goes for your professional and personal life; cut the unnecessary things that only take away energy and time from your life and prioritise the more important stuff.

Leaders Hold Themselves Accountable

Being a leader is a lot of responsibility. As the one in charge, making decisions is going to be part of your responsibilities. You must demonstrate the ability to make the right decisions when time calls for it, and this is no easy feat. Every choice you make has a consequence, an impact on you and the people under your leadership. You must think carefully about every decision you want to make because once the wheels are in motion, you're going to have to stand by your choice. As former businessman Arnold H. Glasgow said:

"A good leader is someone who takes a little more than their fair share of the blame, and a little less than their share of the credit."

That's what it means to be a leader. You're accountable for what you and your followers do. When they struggle, you struggle along with them, and when they succeed, give them the credit and acknowledgement they deserve for a job well done. If they stumble, work with them to see how you can improve.

John Maxwell states that there are five essential reasons for people following a leader:

- ♦ **They Have To** - If you're the boss, they have no choice but to do as they're told.
- ♦ **They Like You** - They follow you because of how they feel about you.
- ♦ **You Deliver** - Your accomplishments speak for themselves, and it has inspired confidence in them.
- ♦ **You Help Them Grow** - They follow you because of what you have done for them and the way you've inspired them to be their best.
- ♦ **Of Who You Are** - They follow you because of who you are, and what you stand for and represent.

Each of these five layers forms a deeper level of commitment. And in today's ever-changing world, it's not enough to be just one or the other anymore. In which layers do you want to be seen? You alone are responsible for achieving that goal.

Leaders Are Great Contributors

People will be looking at you to guide them, and they won't be motivated to do their best if their leader doesn't display the same passion and commitment towards achieving that goal. When a leader is not afraid to roll up his sleeves and *get his hands dirty*, others will follow suit because of the dedication and the desire for getting the job done that is being demonstrated. To earn the respect of your followers, this is how you do it. Without commitment and passion, it's going to be an uphill task for any leader to keep the motivational fire going.

Leaders Are Able to Handle Pressure

A leader who runs around like a chicken with its head cut off whenever a crisis or problem crops up is no leader at all. I don't want to offend anyone, but if you can't handle working under pressure, you shouldn't even try becoming a leader in the first place. Effective leaders are the ones who can *keep a clear head*. You're going to inevitably face some problems along the way, and if you handle them well, your people will begin to trust that you can do this.

Anyone can hold the helm when the sea is calm.
—Publilius Syrus

Leaders Demonstrate Mutual Respect

An effective leader constantly encourages and helps their followers overcome challenges faced without belittling them. Have you ever worked with someone that didn't respect you? If so, I bet your respect towards them wasn't that great either. A leader must respect their followers to gain honour in return. *Respect needs to be earned*, never demanded. When you don't appreciate your followers and vice versa, things can unravel really quickly, and not in a positive way. The best type of leaders and managers are the ones that provide a work environment where employees help each other and value the contributions that everyone makes.

Leaders Are Role Models

You need to be the change you wish to see in the world. If you want to create positive change, it all starts with you and the way you lead others to follow in your footsteps. As a leader, everyone is looking to you for guidance, and it is you that they take their orders from. *Practice what you preach* because your people are watching what you do. If you insist on your team being punctual, you need to ensure that you are punctual too. If you remain calm and cool in stressful situations, your team will do the same. You need to be someone that your team can look up to, admire and respect.

To summarise, all successful leaders:

- o Improve the traits they are lacking
- o Always educate themselves
- o Believe in their abilities
- o Focus on doing things of greater value
- o Hold themselves accountable
- o Are great contributors
- o Are able to handle pressure
- o Demonstrate mutual respect
- o Are role models

Leaders vs. Managers

To evolve into an effective leader, we must understand the difference between leadership and management. I'm working as a so-called "manager" myself, but I know that this is just a designation. Many people don't understand this, and they think leadership and management are synonyms. I say they definitely aren't.

Leaders have a more effective approach to communication rather than controlling. As a leader, you need to have excellent communication skills to explain your vision and tell your team what needs to be done to accomplish a goal. Words are powerful enough to inspire, motivate, and make people push past their boundaries, accomplishing things they never thought possible (we'll talk more about communication in later chapters).

Leaders create followers, and managers manage people and things.

Leaders are focused on taking the organisation from Point A to B. They are also known for taking risks instead of maintaining the status quo and keeping things steady. Leaders try to stretch the organisation past what it's currently doing, thereby growing it bigger and stronger. Leaders are also much more people-focused and relationship-focused. They do more mentoring, coaching or teaching. Leaders have the ability to communicate persuasively, inspiring vision, and getting people excited about the future.

Managers, on the other hand, have more of a control mindset. They are focused on the administration of processes, the structure and the resources of the organisation. They are very task-focused and care most about maintaining the status quo. Maintenance is a key part of what they do. Managers work on the day-to-day tasks and make sure that everything gets done in an orderly fashion.

While managers certainly have a lot of important communication functions, they are more inclined to go with a by-the-book approach. Leaders create followers, and managers manage people and things. That is the easiest way to remember it.

As different as leaders and managers are, both these roles have their importance and purpose; there's no such thing as 100% management or 100% leadership. Sometimes you have to be a good manager as well as a leader, especially if you're in any kind of small business or team setting. Visionary leaders will hire good task-oriented managers to balance out the team. There's only so much you can do as a leader, and you need to understand what your team requires to function better. If your organisation *needs a manager* to help you oversee the team while you handle other affairs, then you need to hire one. As a leader, you can't be afraid to admit when you need help, and you must listen to and consider the needs of your team.

Some great leaders of today exhibit all the leadership qualities needed, and that is why they will always be remembered for their visionary approach. Let's look at (in my opinion) some of the best contemporary leaders. They are all great business leaders, and we can definitely learn something from them.

Jeff Bezos

Jeff Bezos built his empire on a foundation of innovation and experimentation, and his leadership style is mostly known for the customer-first approach and long-term vision. In 1999, Bezos shared his vision for Amazon to become Earth's most customer-centric company where customers will be able to find everything they may want to buy online. This still holds true today. During some meetings, Bezos requests for one chair to be kept empty to represent the Amazon customer. This becomes a constant reminder for the attendees that the customer is the most important person in the room. Bezos' enthusiastic persona (which was compared to a start-up boss trying to make his first payroll) inspires his employees to believe in the vision of Amazon and to make it a reality.

Jack Ma

Ma was never afraid to think outside the box. He decided to start an online business, despite being unable to access the internet in his hometown. After repeatedly changing business models, he founded the e-commerce store Alibaba. Shortly after the foundation, Ma told a journalist: *"We don't want to be number one in China. We want to be number one in the world."* Ever since Alibaba was founded, Ma continues to be a strong advocate of the "think big" approach, which he encourages all his employees to partake in. Leaders are all about change and the willingness to break the rules. For example, Ma persuaded organisations to invest millions of dollars in his company *without* presenting a business plan. Eventually, he pioneered his company to become one of the world's largest businesses online and a renowned name worldwide.

Zhang Ruimin

Ruimin's willingness to be radical with his innovations turned Haier from a small failing company to one of the world's biggest names in household appliances. Ruimin's approach to leadership is to group his employees into smaller teams that manage themselves and even elect their own leaders—a concept that is still unheard of in China and still considered an unusual approach in the Western world. This is exactly what makes Ruimin a great leader. He is willing to take risks and make moves that others are hesitant to do.

Howard Schultz

The CEO of Starbucks is considered ahead of most CEO's because he understood that he wasn't selling a product.

Schultz knew that he was selling an *experience* to the customer. His concept involved inviting décor, calming music and speedy Wi-Fi so everyone would feel at home. He was able to imagine Starbucks as a place that was the most-visited after home and work, whereas other food/drink stops adopt the grab-and-go approach. Schultz saw the value in focusing beyond only the sales numbers and creating a pleasant environment for the customer.

Unlike a manager who leads with completion, a leader chooses to lead with empathy and connection. You could decide to go with the dictatorial approach to leadership, and that may get things done, but that won't make you a great leader. The question is, do you want to be a leader people *have* to work for or do you want to be a leader people *want* to work for? Being an effective leader means you need to put yourself in your team's shoes and understand their concerns. With that understanding, you're one step closer to making a difference in their lives and performance.

CHAPTER 2:

How (Not) to Become A Leader

Leadership is unlocking people's potential to
become better.   —BILL BRADLEY

*L*eadership is like a double-edged sword. Do it well, and you could achieve unimaginable greatness, leaving behind a legacy that lasts a lifetime. Do it badly, and you'll be remembered for all the wrong reasons. What's worse, poor leadership on your part could lead to a bad team dynamic which ends in you losing some of the best talents in your organisation. So, how do we prevent bad leadership? And what can we do to become successful leaders instead? After looking at the basic principles of leadership, it's now time for you to actively build the most essential characteristics that leaders have. In this chapter, I've laid out some qualities you have to develop and more importantly, the ones you want to steer clear from in order to evolve into an effective leader. When you successfully acquire these skills, you'll be able to move onto the next step and establish a workplace every team member dreams of.

The Cost of Poor Leadership

There is no such thing as a bad team—only a bad leader. If right now, your team is not stepping up, it could be because you are not leading them to step up. For example, if you have a toxic person in your team that sabotages the whole organisation, you need to fire that person. Bad leaders inflict an air of superiority over their people, and they will never succeed in their role because no one will ever respect a leader who makes it difficult to be likeable. Remember, like the trunk, you want to be supportive, not superior. When you choose not to be humble, you lose self-awareness, and become blinded to your own faults.

Leadership sets the tone for *everything* in an organisation. The culture, the standards, the performance, and the outcomes—all lead back to leadership. An environment with poor leadership becomes soulless. People forget why they started working for the company in the first place. You will know that you're probably guilty of being a lousy leader if your team disperses as soon as you arrive. No leader is perfect, but if you want to become an effective leader, you must avoid the following leadership mistakes.

You Have No Vision

While several mistakes contribute to poor leadership style, the number one factor why you fail as a leader is because you lack a compelling vision.

Where there is no vision, the people perish.

A vision helps you define the kind of reputation you want your business to be associated with and where you see yourself in the future. What kind of impression do you want to leave? What do you want to be remembered for? You have to set the idea, connect everyone to that mission, inspire people to collaborate, and elevate themselves to a new standard of performance. A lack of vision equals failure every single time. Your people want to see progress. They want to know that their efforts and hard work are paying off, and they are moving forward, but a leader without a vision is someone who cannot provide these things for their people. Find something they can aspire towards. It can be something simple—your vision doesn't have to be as huge as Jack Ma's (becoming the world's largest e-commerce store), but you should work towards it with the same passion and drive.

A Lack of Integrity

Once your followers figure out who you are (and it won't take them long to) and realise you lack integrity and transparency, you're not going to remain in the leadership position for very long. No one likes a shady leader or someone that they feel they cannot trust. Trust and respect go a long way in successful and effective leadership, and if your team doesn't respect you or trust you as a leader, your team will be doomed right from the start with no hope of success.

Become the kind of leader that people would follow voluntarily; even if you had no title or position.
—Brian Tracy

Overthinking

A simple matter that could be resolved easily could get blown out of proportion if a leader reacts to it in a highly emotional way. One of the reasons people generally become more sensitive than they should is because they tend to overthink a lot of things. Avoid overthinking situations and just *see things for what they are* (any Stoics here?). Look at the facts in front of you, and if something is not an objective fact, then don't think about it. Observe the situation, don't embellish, don't assume, and don't add on "facts" of your own. This is how things get more complicated than they should, and emotions get fired up when there is no need for them to.

Thinking You Have All the Answers

It's just as bad as overthinking. A leader who thinks they have all the answers is a leader who is missing out on a great learning opportunity. Even if you believe that you do have all the answers, and maybe you do, you should still listen to what your team or anyone who approaches you with a suggestion or solution has to say. Great leaders are *willing to listen.* Bad leaders brush others off and insist on things being done their way. Do that, and you'll never discover if there was indeed a better way you could have taken; an approach that would have opened the door to new possibilities and opportunities.

Not Broadening Your Perspective

In the increasingly globalised world today, leadership's evolution has risen onto a new plateau. Do you want to enter the team floor? Then you have to *be open-minded,* now more than ever. An effective leader who has a broader view of the world develops the ability to see things from multiple points of view, making better, informed decisions to ensure the best possible outcome. One of the biggest mistakes you could make as a leader would be to confine your circle to only people who talk, act, speak, and look like you do. Not only is this strategically ineffective but also extremely boring, so please don't do this. We will discuss more about diversity in Chapter 3.

Good leadership requires you to surround yourself with people of diverse perspectives who can disagree with you without fear of retaliation. —Doris Kearns Goodwin

A Lack of Love

Disney's Ratatouille movie brought to light an interesting concept: a leader can come from anywhere, even a rat with a dream and a *passion*. Leadership, by definition, isn't about trying to do something great as a lone ranger. It's about inspiring others to share the dream, and then creating circumstances where they can do their absolute best work. This is impossible to achieve if the leaders themselves lack passion and heart. Today, we are not in Business-to-Customer or Business-to-Business businesses. We are in the *People-to-People* business.

We are there to serve people. You have to communicate with love, and this is the best-kept secret of successful leaders: to love what you do, remain in love with your leadership role, staying in love with your people, staying in love with your customers, staying in love with your organisation, and coming from the right place. Understanding your team members on a deep heartfelt level, always doing the right thing, treating your employees like family members. That's what authentic leadership is.

A great leader's courage to fulfill his vision comes from passion, not position. —John Maxwell

Your Team Is Not Comfortable Around You

Do you enjoy working with someone you don't feel comfortable around? I wouldn't think so, and you can't expect your team to feel any different. Employees leave if they have a weak leader at the helm of the ship, no matter how much they love their jobs. Your followers need to be comfortable enough to voice their opinions and concerns. For example, if they are having difficulty working with another member of their team, they need to feel comfortable enough to approach you and bring up those concerns without worrying about repercussions. As a leader, you need to establish yourself as a trustworthy figure and *encourage an open-door policy* among the people you are managing, helping them and making them feel safe whenever they approach you with a problem.

Before we continue, I wanted to emphasize the importance of understanding all these mistakes. Becoming a great leader sets the foundation of the whole team dynamic, and if you don't accomplish this first step, all future efforts will be worthless. Ask yourself right now, am I guilty of doing these things? If yes, start working on them. If no, perfect! In this regard, here are a few more mistakes you should be aware of.

Leaders aren't born, they are made. And they are made just like anything else, through hard work. And that's the price we'll have to pay to achieve that goal, or any goal.
—*Vince Lombardi*

Overworking Your Team

Overworking the best employees on the team is how you burn them out. Unfortunately, this is something weak leaders are guilty of because they become too comfortable relying on the most dependable members of their team. While the hardworking, performing team members no doubt should be praised, if you pile on too much work on them, they will start harbouring negative energy and find themselves feeling tired or burned out. And in my experience, a burned-out employee accomplishes as much as a sloth.

A Lack of Resources

Are you providing your team with everything that they need? *Do you equip them for success?* When a leader fails to provide adequate resources for a team to be successful, the group as a whole is going to fail. It is the leader's job to provide funding, technology, resources, influence staffing, and whatever else is needed for projects and operational responsibilities to be considered successful.

Valuing Profits More Than People

The minute a leader and an organisation start to value their bottom line more than the people who work hard for them is when the best employees pack up and leave. Sir Richard Branson (Head of Virgin Group Ltd.) is one leader who is famous for his *"people first" approach* and for ensuring his team is always happy in their jobs. He says that if you don't look after your employees, your company gets sad. People can feel this, and it leads to a negative customer experience.

Your team is more than just resources that were hired to get the job done for you. They are people too. Treating your team as a means to an end is what bad leaders do. They shouldn't even be called leaders if this is the approach that they resort to. When you don't recognise your people's value and contribution, you fail to motivate them, and once an employee has had enough, they'll hand in their resignation.

A man who wants to lead the orchestra must turn his back on the crowd. —Max Lucado

Failing to Delegate

A bad leader will try to do it all because they believe they can do it better and realise too late that they should have delegated their tasks after all. Failure to entrust and spread the work evenly among your team, playing to each member's strengths, is one of the costs of poor leadership. And who ends up paying the price for it? The team; they fail to meet deadlines, and the job is not done as well as it could have been.

Part of being an effective leader is knowing the *strengths and weaknesses of your team members* and then behaving in a way that draws all of their positive qualities together. As a great leader, you need to delegate the right job to the right people, so they produce excellent results because they know exactly what to do when a task is given to them. People have been known to become better performers and become more engaged when they feel they are really excelling at the tasks at hand, and you would be surprised at just how much this can impact the productivity of a team.

To do great things is difficult; but to command great things is more difficult. —Friedrich Nietzsche

Being Slow to Act and Adapt

The fear of making mistakes could be one of the traits that turn a potentially good leader into a bad one. Decisions need to be made quickly and sometimes on the spot, depending on the challenge you're faced with. And if you are too slow or too afraid to make a move quickly enough to stay one step ahead, you will always find yourself two steps behind everybody else. Especially in today's fast-changing world, adapting is one of the most crucial qualities of a successful company. You don't have to learn it the hard way like many organisations did. Nokia, for example, was the global leader in mobile phones in the 1990s. However, they got run over by Apple and Samsung because they failed to upgrade and adapt their phones to new discoveries like the internet or touch screens abilities.

Forgetting to Focus on The Customer

When you fail to pay attention to what the needs of your customers are, you are destined for failure. It's not only the employees that leaders need to focus on, but it's the customers too—the people who help to keep the business alive, besides the employees. A customer is *the financial lifeline of the company*, and when your customers are gone, so are you. A leader who excels at what they do thinks about the customer experience more than the bottom line. Ask yourself, *"How can I inspire loyalty and satisfaction among the customer, the same way I try to do for my team?".* Ignoring the needs of others is the quickest way to ensure that your days in that leadership position are numbered. Do you remember how Jeff Bezos orders one chair empty to represent the customer? This is exactly how much you should value your customers.

In short, avoid these mistakes to become an effective leader:

- o   Having no vision
- o   A lack of integrity
- o   Overthinking
- o   Thinking you have all the answers
- o   Not broadening your perspective
- o   A lack of love
- o   Not making your team comfortable around you
- o   Overworking your team
- o   A lack of resources
- o   Valuing profits more than people
- o   Failing to delegate
- o   Being slow to act and adapt
- o   Forgetting to focus on the customer

The Charm of Great Leadership

Now that you know the characteristics you should avoid, let's look at the qualities you must develop to become a successful team leader. It starts with the ability to be introspective. Introspection allows you to reflect on your actions thus far and the contributions you've made—how you've influenced others, what your goals are, and what purposeful role you may play in their life at this point.

Introspection forces you to confront what's happening within you internally, so you can no longer deny or ignore all the thoughts and emotions you may have tried to run away from for so long. In doing so, you become enlightened, and you can free yourself from the shackles of ignorance. Take hold of this introspection and unfold the following qualities that will turn you into an effective leader, and people will be more than happy to follow.

Have Courage

You must be willing to take risks to reach your goals even if you're not guaranteed success. There is no certainty in life or business. Every commitment and action you make will always entail some kind of risk or consequence. In your leadership, there are going to be moments that push you beyond your limits, moments that challenge you and threaten to defeat you, testing your will to see what you're made of. For this reason, you must develop courage and inner strength to weather the storm and still exhibit self-control and positivity despite the difficulties. But how can we have more courage? Personally, if I find myself in such a position where I run into adversities, I remember that it's times like these that give us the opportunity to grow and strengthen our personality.

Treat Your People Like Unique Individuals

It's easy to think of your team as a whole unit, forgetting that each member of the group is a unique individual in their own right. They all have a different perspective, approach, and unique view, each one with something to offer if you know how to recognise their individual contributions and strengths. To be an effective leader that solves problems for good, you need to tailor your solutions according to the person you are dealing with. Although two people may face a similar problem, the way that they approach or handle the problem will be very different because they are two diverse personalities. The issue will be perceived individually and, as such, affect them differently in the process. Treat them as individuals *first* and a team second.

Be Humble

Humility is going to be one of your greatest traits as a leader. Great leaders are decisive and strong, yet humble at the same time. Humility is not a weakness or a lack of self-confidence. It means that you have the courage and awareness needed to recognise the strength and value others have, and you don't feel threatened about it. As a great leader, you have to encourage and nurture the talent surrounding you, even if it means there could be some who ends up being better than you are. Never let your ego get in the way! Why? Because a good leader understands that it is not about them, it is about the organisation as a whole and everyone involved. Be humble because it is okay to admit your mistakes. It is okay to admit you don't have all the answers.

The challenge of leadership is to be strong, but not rude; be kind, but not weak; be bold, but not bully; be thoughtful, but not lazy; be humble, but not timid; be proud, but not arrogant; have humor, but without folly.
—Jim Rohn

Give Your Team a Purpose

As already mentioned, great leaders *must have a vision*. This is a non-negotiable quality that cannot be compromised. You must be able to look ahead, be clear, and excited about the idea of where you're going and what you're trying to accomplish. Like a general in war, leaders hone their strategic planning skills to turn this vision into reality. They rise each morning with a sense of purpose, and they pass this purpose on to their team. This will keep your team's motivation going.

If you are anything like me, you need a reason to be motivated at doing something. I wash the dishes because they'll be clean afterwards, I eat vegetables so that my body is healthy, I write this book to help as many people as possible become better team leaders. In fact, we humans love to know why we should do things. So, give your team a reason to come to work every day, show them how their work contributes to the organisation's goals, and tell them the impact of these goals. Employees can only commit 100% when they can connect the things they do to the end goal, especially during the most difficult moments. When you have a clear reason for doing what you're doing, you're never in doubt, and you always know why you must persevere.

Prioritise and Plan

Being able to prioritise enables you to have a clear sense of direction, and it always ensures that the most important things don't slip through the. Which one is your priority? Make lists, and then highlight the important points. Successful leaders rarely ever do things on a whim. To stay on track, priorities need to be set, and work needs to get done according to those priorities. That's the only way to go about it. Every thought, action, and decision must be carefully mapped out and planned down to the last detail.

This is how you achieve more productivity, stay focused on what you need to do, and remain motivated to accomplish your goals. Leaders always exhibit a lot of organisation and planning in their day because they know they are responsible for other individuals; they know people are looking towards them to lead the way.

A leader takes people where they want to go. A great leader takes people where they don't necessarily want to go, but ought to be. —Rosalynn Carter

Don't Be Afraid to Ask Questions

As already mentioned, being a leader doesn't mean you have to know everything. Questions give you the answers you need, and you should never feel awkward or embarrassed about having questions on your mind. Part of the greatness of a leader is the ability to take other people's advice and appreciate when someone is able to present a solution. This isn't something that all leaders can do. A leader who is willing to ask questions will *always* be a better leader than someone who pretends to know it all. The latter will usually end up being too bossy and domineering instead of empowering.

Listen To Your Team

Listening to what your team needs is the easiest way to decide what to do. Not only will you know what to improve on, but you will also make your team feel more acknowledged. If you were an employee, would you want a leader who is open and willing to listen to your needs? Or would you prefer a leader who dismisses your ideas as soon as you bring them up? Be a good listener, and not just listen for the sake of doing so. You need to listen actively and really pay attention to what your team has to say and what they need from you. You are the one they will go to when they feel something needs to be improved. When your people know that their leader is taking their every concern seriously, no matter how small it may be, they will feel appreciated, which will motivate them to perform better.

Therefore, in order to become a successful team leader, you must:

- o   Have courage
- o   Treat your people like unique individuals
- o   Be humble
- o   Give your team a purpose
- o   Prioritise and plan
- o   Don't be afraid to ask questions
- o   Listen to your team

A dynamic, hardworking, successful team runs like a well-oiled machine. Every cog to the wheel of your team enters smoothly into its gear to achieve a harmonious result. That can only happen under the helm of great leadership; it occurs through the actions and decisions you decide to (or not to) make. But this kind of team dynamic doesn't happen by default. It is something you need to *create by design*.

Step II:
Create a Productive Work Environment

CHAPTER 3:

Why Diversity is Essential

A diverse mix of voices leads to better discussions, decisions, and outcomes for everyone.
—SUNDAR PICHAI

*D*iversity is a subject that is not talked about enough at the workplace. The world is evolving rapidly, and yet, we are not embracing inclusion at the same pace. Diversity and discrimination are major issues that can cause a lot of problems at the workplace if they are not addressed adequately by leaders. Why the leaders? Because the leaders are the ones who set the example for others to follow.

We are all different, and our differences can generate various points of view contributing to increased creativity and innovation. Yet, many team leaders and businesses are not capitalising on this tremendous opportunity when choosing to either overlook or ignore the importance of diversity in today's work environments. In my time with top leaders, I have found that many fail to see that by embracing different talents, appreciating each member, and providing inclusive leadership, they can utilise the differences to achieve the overall goals and objectives better.

The Unspoken Problem

Our cities are changing. Our work environments and even the way we work is changing. But what's not changing enough is diversity and inclusion. Men still <u>outnumber</u> women when it comes to leading organisations. In fact, according to <u>research,</u> in the United States alone, more men named John are leaders of major companies than women leaders overall (isn't that crazy?). There is also another problem the workplace faces, and that is institutionalised racism. It is <u>well-documented</u> that if you have a name that sounds foreign, you have a harder time getting a job outside your country of origin. Yes, name discrimination exists, and it is a genuine problem that nobody likes to talk about.

Unconscious bias in the workplace is just that— unconscious. It occurs before we realise it, and it negatively shapes our judgement of people, especially when it comes to important decisions, like hiring, promoting, and developing talent. Due to its subtlety, unconscious bias leads to unintentional exclusion. But you can influence change by first *becoming aware* of these prejudices and then *exposing yourself* to more diversity.

As a leader, you have the unique opportunity to open yourself up to new ways of doing things to lead inclusively. Mentor someone different from you. Give an assignment to someone other than your average go-to person. When promoting, think about who has made contributions that you've overlooked. Ask the shy or introverted employee for input during a meeting, get to know someone different by asking them to lunch, or speak up when you hear inappropriate or disrespectful comments said in your presence. Don't assume the answer; ask questions to understand points of view that are different from yours. Monitor yourself and observe when your biases get in the way. You could do so many things to bring about change once you recognise the reasons for encouraging diversity.

Not only is it the *right* thing to do, but also because from a strategic standpoint, it is one of the most *useful* things you can do. According to several <u>studies</u> and <u>research,</u> boosting diversity in the company can make it more successful. For instance, researchers at McKinsey found that racially diverse teams outperform the non-diverse teams by <u>35%</u>.

We have a very diverse environment and a very inclusive culture and those characteristics got us through the tough times. Diversity generated a better strategy, better risk management, better debates, and better outcomes.
—Alan Joyce

When I first learnt about diversity, I was puzzled. I don't consider myself a small-minded person, but in the beginning, trying to create a diverse team didn't make sense to me. I thought that people would only get into disputes and would not be able to work with one another, and you're probably thinking the same thing right now. Nonetheless, I started to create teams of diverse people I wouldn't normally put together. And the results were surprisingly good. Once we understand how diversity at the workplace works, we can start using it to our advantage while also making everyone else happier.

What Workplace Diversity Means

Many leaders don't approach diversity in the right way and with the right mindset. Studies show that forced diversity training could backfire negatively. It makes people feel resentful and increases prejudice. Many people suddenly think that if you're a minority or from a different background, you're getting opportunities handed to you not because you deserved them but because a company was simply trying to fill its diversity quota. People are quick to attribute it to tokenism or diversity schemes. For example, believing you only got the job because you're a woman or from a different race.

Real, truthful workplace diversity happens when a company embraces a wide range of factors that make individuals unique. This includes culture, race, age, religion, gender, social status, personality, and even sexual orientation. It's more than just acknowledging the diversity of a population; it means to value all the things about a person that makes them unique. Don't force it, but start to genuinely appreciate the different qualities of each person.

Inclusivity means not just we're allowed to be there, but we are valued. I've always said: smart teams will do amazing things, but truly diverse teams will do impossible things. —Claudia Brind-Woody

Why Does Diversity Matter?

Leaders need to make a commitment—a commitment to being consciously inclusive. They need to take the responsibility of respecting differences, being accountable and embracing possibilities. Imagine the impact you could have if you chose to go with that approach. Diversity in the workplace promotes a positive working environment—an environment in which your employees will grow and thrive because no one feels excluded, left out, or out of place. When employees work with people from different backgrounds, they have a unique opportunity in their hands. They get the chance to learn from one another. In doing so, they are able to produce higher quality products and services.

Building a diverse team is important. No doubt, a varied group does come with its own set of challenges. But you'll find more challenges in a team that consists of all like-minded individuals. The scope of thinking is severely limited because when every person thinks of a problem in the same way, no different solutions can be found. Diversity brings together people from various aspects of society, race, gender, and backgrounds in one organisation. It is a strategy you can use for better productivity and growth in the years ahead.

Globalisation is on the rise, family and social arrangements are evolving, and company structures are changing rapidly. Diverse work environments are unavoidable, and some companies find themselves changing almost naturally to accommodate those needs. Employees can now work remotely, internationally, full-time or part-time, belong to several generations, and more. Diversity in teams comes with challenges, but in my opinion, the benefits outweigh the struggles. Having a strong team of employees who can learn from different cultures, backgrounds, and skillsets is one of those benefits. Becoming better collaborators and communicators is another along with better problem-solving. There is a lot to be gained from incorporating diversity.

A Boost in Creativity

Have you ever had a discussion with someone that has a totally different viewpoint than you? Didn't it make you look at things from a different angle, one that you wouldn't have thought of otherwise? With different perspectives in the team, *no stone is left unturned* when solutions are explored. Bouncing ideas off people who think and view the world differently from you can open your eyes to new possibilities and make you see things in a way you never have before.

This, in turn, will encourage your team members to be more creative in their thinking as they work together to figure out how to come up with the best possible solutions.

Diversity and inclusion, which are the real grounds for creativity, must remain at the center of what we do.
—Marco Bizzarri

It Promotes Innovation

Innovation comes from the conflicts that will undoubtedly arise when a team consists of diverse backgrounds. But as you sit there and listen to various types of people with different ideas, you will have the opportunity to create innovation for your products or services by *combining these ideas.* This encourages responsibility and emboldens the employees to contribute individually. New ideas are born, and the gaps in your business are filled. Your organisation thus gains a competitive advantage, leading to better market share and growth.

Expand Your Talent Pool

A diverse talent pool means that employees from all different backgrounds, skillsets, and experiences come together for a common goal.

When you broaden your net, you get the best fish in the sea.

The team also becomes more well-rounded, benefitting from these various perspectives, ideas, and inputs. Once people see that the organisation is a globally accepting firm, you will attract a diverse range of employees to work in your environment. People will want to work for your business when they realise it doesn't practice employment discrimination.

It Encourages Team Unity

Showing your team that your business is a source of acceptance to all differences makes them feel more trusted, respected, and allows strong friendships to grow among the entire team. *Team morale* gets a boost as employees come together despite the differences in ideas and perspectives. The team and company culture improve, and you significantly increase your chances of retaining the best talents in the industry, especially millennials who value workplace diversity.

We have become not a melting pot but a beautiful mosaic.
—Jimmy Carter

Your Customer Base Becomes Equally as Diverse

Showing that you understand diversity and, more importantly, *support* diversity will help you attract a different and equally diverse customer base, made up of different types of customers. More customers mean more and better business opportunities. It also improves your business's reputation because when your employees are thriving in their jobs, they will speak positively about your organisation. And word of mouth can be a very effective marketing approach to take.

By combining diverse cultures and experiences, you will have a broad understanding of what the consumer needs. Your connection with your clients is strengthened, and you show them that your business has many shared interests with them. It gives them something to relate to.

Expanding Worldwide Becomes Easier

Being diverse means you're able to communicate well with people hailing from various parts of the world, which will help you win them over and dramatically increase your market share. A varied team knows how to form relationships and understands the nuances between different cultures, making it easier for your business to conquer the local markets in different regions.

Doing business abroad requires a thorough understanding of the local workforce. When you have team members who come from the country you're expanding to, the insight and knowledge that comes with it could be invaluable to your expansion. Moreover, diversity is crucial for an organisation's ability to innovate and adapt in a fast-changing environment. When you have variety in the workplace, your business is more open to the world and ready to grow.

A Team with a Dynamically Diverse Working Style

Keeping your team motivated, enthusiastic, and on their toes is easy when you bring together minds and personalities that think, act, and behave differently. Diversity *keeps things interesting* because you never know what new idea is going to come up next. As the leader, it allows you to watch how your team interacts with people of different backgrounds. And you'll be able to keep an eye out for the employee who displays the qualities of a potential leader in the making.

We are all different, which is great because we are all unique. Without diversity, life would be very boring.
—Catherine Pulsifer

To summarise, these are the reasons why you should implement diversity at your workplace:

- o Your team gets a boost in creativity
- o It promotes innovation
- o You can expand your talent pool
- o It encourages team unity
- o Your customer base becomes equally as diverse
- o Expanding worldwide becomes easier
- o The team develops a dynamically diverse working style

In an advertising agency in London, a group of five creative directors got together and initiated the Great British Diversity Experiment. They enlisted 120 people who came from various backgrounds. These individuals were put into teams and asked to solve problems. The researchers studied them ethnographically, analysing them and observed the way they interacted in comparison to a homogenous group. They found that diverse groups were the more creative ones because they had access to more perspectives with all the different people involved. This kind of an environment makes you connect the dots in different ways. Diversity is beneficial. It's not about political correctness, and it's not about the mathematical proof for variety. The world is changing, and it always will keep changing. Companies must learn to evolve and change with the times or risk becoming extinct.

The Challenges of a Diverse Workforce

As great as it is to see people from all walks of life come together to create, innovate, brainstorm, and share their unique perspectives while working together as a team, diversity also comes with some challenges. The most obvious issue with a diverse team is that some members may be native speakers of another language. They may not be bilingual and struggle to be well-versed in another. Not understanding each other's languages can lead to communication barriers and culture clashes, which are common when multiple cultures come together. This has a direct impact on the team's workflow and performance.

The problem with a too diverse team is that there's an increased tendency for employees to indulge in interpersonal conflicts. As different beliefs, values, traditions, norms and opinions come together, the chance of disagreements increases. This leads to increased opportunities for employees to argue about non-work related topics, varying from serious to trivial ones.

Regardless of the cause, such conflicts result in the development of negative emotions in a team, slower decision-making and lost productivity.

Another challenge you'll find is that people with different interests and values may struggle to connect. Without a common ground, it's not easy to start an exciting conversation, and therefore, it's hard to build a relationship. People don't work as well when they have no connection with the other team members, which will reflect in the overall performance.

You need to cultivate a team that maximises benefits and overcomes challenges more than anything else. Instead of letting these challenges hold the organisation back, you need to set the example of embracing diversity and encouraging your team to be comfortable with change. However, diversity can also backfire if the challenges become more of a hindrance than a benefit. That's why it's your job to find the perfect balance between diversity and comfort.

We know that diversity can sometimes be more uncomfortable because things are less familiar – but it gets the best results. —Megan Smith

How to Encourage Greater Diversity

The time for change is always now—not tomorrow, not next week, next month, or a year from now, it's now. We shouldn't wait for the "right time" to make a move for the better. We should seize the day and the opportunity when it comes. So, how can you develop more diversity at the workplace? There is a lot that can be done as a team, a leader, and an organisation as a whole. For example, if you're handling the recruitment process, consider ways to minimise your unconscious bias.

In the 1970s and 1980s, the symphony orchestra in the United States was made up of all white men. They decided to hold blind auditions to do something about that. Musicians auditioned behind the screen so the person in charge of hiring couldn't tell if it was a man or woman, or what the colour of their skin was. The result of this approach was that the number of women getting accepted into orchestras increased to between 25 - 46%. A company called GapJumpers took this idea of blind auditions and applied it to the corporate world. Instead of looking through CVs to screen their candidates, they assigned challenges anonymously. As a result, there were 60% more minority applicants selected for interviews. Turns out, not being able to find the "best candidate" was not the issue at all. The problem was that the best candidates were often overlooked due to unconscious bias.

Another example of what can be done to address diversity is to say something, even if nobody says anything. Nothing changes if we all keep silent. So, if you are in a room, in a meeting, in a company, speaking with your team or co-workers, talk about diversity and inclusion, and show that you're aware of what's going on.

Unity, not uniformity, must be our aim. We attain unity only through variety. Differences must be integrated, not annihilated, not absorbed. —Mary Parker Follett

A great team leader leverages the strengths of its members and uses those strengths to offset any weaknesses. The leader knows that an employee is so much more than just the job that they are doing. They are unique, interesting individuals with their own set of talents, skills, and knowledge that opens the team up to a wealth of new opportunities.

Let go of the emotions and preconceived notions or judgments that impede your progress and embrace more diversity at the workplace by doing these things:

- Challenge yourself
- Encourage a culture of openness
- Highlight diversity
- Work on improving your social skills
- Keep an open mind and listen with one too
- Encourage team empathy
- Allow flexible work hours
- Ensure social activities are inclusive

Here's a quick reminder: the most important aspect of the concepts I share here is YOU. Ask yourself, how could I do that? How is this applicable to me? Which projects would this work for? Don't read this content without delving into the ideas. Always think of (and write down) ways to implement these strategies yourself. That being said, let's take a look at how you can encourage greater diversity.

Challenge Yourself

Instead of looking at the common ground among your employees, start looking for the differences. Focus on that during your thought process and encourage your team to reflect on working with someone who is from a different background than they are. For example, when you are working together on a project with your team, at the start of the project, encourage them to share what they think *makes them different* and how this strength can benefit the outcome of the project.

This is also an opportunity for you, the leader, to observe whether there is too much of the same kind of thinking taking place because you subconsciously put together a team of people who thought the same way you did. If that's the case, then this is your opportunity to take corrective action by including more diversity moving forward. The first step in addressing a problem is first to acknowledge that there is a problem.

Encourage a Culture of Cohesiveness

When employees feel like they might be the odd one out and don't belong, they will not have the confidence to speak up and share their ideas. It is the leader's responsibility to encourage openness so plans can be discussed freely. For this to happen, *respect* is one of the major key principles that absolutely must be present. An effective leader consistently inspires and helps their people overcome challenges faced without depreciating them. So, provide a work environment where employees help each other and value the contributions that everyone makes. This way, they will *want to* give their input, even if it might be an unusual one.

Diversity is being invited to the party; inclusion is being asked to dance. —Verna Myers

Highlight Diversity

Talk about it, mention it in the job ads that you post when recruiting potential new employees, encourage your team to refer to other potential employees from groups that may be underrepresented and reward them for it. Create guidelines at work that are diversity-friendly. During the interview process, have a diverse panel for greater equality and fairness. For example, Canadian Prime Minister Justin Trudeau knocked it out of the park when he put together a diverse team as part of his Cabinet. In doing so, he achieved diversity, inclusion, and equality. All decisions that are going to be made now and, in the future, will be a reflection of those different minds coming together.

Work on Improving Your Social Skills

Communication and social skills promote cultural diversity. Today's workplace is a melting pot of diverse cultures and languages. For everyone to be able to work in harmony, it is crucial to have good social skills. As a leader, you should encourage your team to work on improving their social skills too. Social skills lend to a strong social presence, and in the career world where connections and networking matter most, *being able to socialise is an invaluable resource*. It makes it easier to build productive, cohesive teams and work well together to get things done.

Social skills help you maintain positive and amicable relationships with your co-workers, regardless of how different your backgrounds may be. You are going to spend most of your day working with them, and without the proper social skills on hand, it can be difficult to build and construct productive relationships. How can you develop your social skills? We will discuss that in chapter 6.

Keep an Open Mind and Listen with One Too

If you listen with an open mind, you will be more receptive to what you are hearing. Being judgmental or opinionated can disrupt your efforts to encourage unity and harmony among your followers. Judgement is a poor use of time that distracts and weakens our focus. Everyone has a story to tell, and there is always something you can learn from someone who is different from you—*always be a student*. Encourage open-mindedness and the willingness to listen receptively among your team by demonstrating your desire to do the same. Lead by example.

When we listen and celebrate what is both common and different, we become a wiser, more inclusive, and better organization. —Pat Wadors

Encourage Team Empathy

Encourage the entire team to put themselves in their colleague's shoes and try to feel every emotion that they do —the joy, sadness, distress, frustration, happiness, anger, whatever they may be feeling, especially if there is someone new to the team. Sometimes we forget that the ones who seem on the outs are struggling and trying their best to fit in, and it's much harder to do that when they don't feel welcomed by their team. It can be a very demoralising and unhappy experience. Being empathic needs focus and concentration, but the effort will be worth it when you see how well your team comes together as soon as more empathy is at play.

Through empathy, your listening abilities improve because you immerse yourself in the world of another. You start to pay a little bit more attention to the way someone else feels. This skill is at the core of what it means to be a great leader and listener, someone people love talking and pouring their hearts out to.

Allow Flexible Work Hours

For your employees, the ability to work from home, have flexible work hours, or job sharing can be the difference between having to give up their job or being able to continue contributing their skills to the team. This is especially true if they have other commitments they are trying to balance with work. Does it matter if they are physically in the office or not? In my opinion, as long as your employee is getting the job done, it doesn't. What does matter is whether you can count on them and *trust them*. Flexible work environments make it easier for employees who have had to go on an extended break, like maternity leave, for example, to ease back into the work structure.

Ensure Social Activities Are Inclusive

Some activities organised by the company might not be suitable for all employees. For instance, holding a team get-together session over dinner and drinks will not be the best activity for an employee who may be a recovering alcoholic, on medication, or someone who needs to drive quite a distance to get back home. You have to consider more inclusive alternatives when planning office and team after-work activities. Of course, that is not to say that a group of friends can't go out after work and enjoy a few drinks together. Rather, this is about ensuring that the activities planned are thought of *with everyone in mind*, and not just a selected group of individuals.

Employees who work and play together, stay together as a team. Personally, I love bonding with my team outside of work, and it's an important relationship-building exercise. It helps everyone to enjoy each other's company without thinking about work for a change, and that bond of friendship will carry over and fuel their motivation when it's crunch time again.

When everyone is included, everyone wins.
—Jesse Jackson

You will encourage more diversity at your workplace if you:

- o Challenge yourself
- o Encourage a culture of cohesiveness
- o Highlight diversity
- o Improve your social skills
- o Keep an open mind
- o Encourage team empathy
- o Allow flexible work hours
- o Ensure social activities are inclusive

Hopefully, after reading this chapter, you are fully motivated to diversify your teams. But before you start turning your organisation upside down, you need to remember that having a too diverse team could be detrimental. The most important aspect of teamwork is that your team members can enjoy working together. If people don't get along well, it's hard to create something collectively. Nevertheless, don't get discouraged by that because, as we've seen, having different viewpoints and opinions may lead to conflicts, but the outcome will be all the better for it. The key is to start being more aware of diversity, then slowly implementing it into your team dynamic and finding the perfect balance. It takes some practice to find the sweet spot of a creative and harmonious team, but it's definitely worth it.

CHAPTER 4:

Is Your Team Having Fun?

I think Smithers picked me because of my
motivational skills. Everyone says they have to work
a lot harder when I'm around.   —HOMER SIMPSON

*G*rowing and nurturing a diverse team is going to be a new experience for many leaders. While you're focused on efficiency and ensuring that everyone on the team is getting along well and doing what they are supposed to, there's another vital aspect you need to pay attention to: *Are they having fun?*

This is my favourite part of the process. I mean, who doesn't enjoy having fun? It is a common misconception that "having fun at work" means the employees are slacking off and not doing their duties, but it is important to note that fun can come in several forms. The old perception of "having fun" should be dismissed because enjoying a day at work does not mean that responsibilities are being neglected. A good team leader knows it is imperative to create the workday as engaging as possible so the employees don't feel that the day is dragging by. People should actually enjoy coming into the office and avoid the dreaded *Sunday Gloom* when they know Monday is approaching.

When It's All Work and No Play

I bet you know at least one person who dreads going into work and hates their job. They are miserable and frequently complain about how much they hate being at the office and can't wait for the day they get to leave. If it isn't them who hates their job, it's their colleague at the office who looks unhappy as they type away behind the desk. They come to work, clock in, and clock out for the sake of taking home a paycheck, and that's about it. There is no joy, motivation or passion, and worst of all, not an ounce of happiness. Coming to work for them almost feels like a prison sentence, something they are forced to do because they have to earn a living. Maybe at some point, you have felt that way before you found yourself in a leadership position.

Here are several reasons why employees could be feeling this way:

- There is no element of play or fun in the tasks that they have to handle.
- They are stressed.
- They don't feel supported.
- They don't feel like they have any connections or good relationships with anyone at the office.
- They are not living up to their full potential.
- They don't see a goal or have a vision of the direction they are going towards.
- They don't see any room for growth in their current organisation.

Considering that about <u>one-third</u> of an employee's life is spent at work, that is a lot of time to spent unhappy. *90,000* hours of your life, to be precise, are spent at your job, and if you don't enjoy what you do, you are going to spend a third of your life feeling miserable and dreading every single minute. So, how do you protect your team from such an awful work life?

Employees feel disengaged and demotivated at work when they don't feel challenged enough. Yes, it isn't *fun* that is going to make them slack off; it's *not being challenged.*

When employees don't feel challenged, they can become bored, disengaged, and even complacent. Almost every leader or manager has experienced that dreaded moment when an employee asks to speak to them privately. They walk into the office, and once the doors are shut, the employee hands in their letter of resignation. More than once, the leader has found themselves feeling taken aback or even shocked, especially when the letter happens to come from one of their best employees. They often don't see this move coming and ask the employee, *"Why are you leaving? Were you not happy here?"*. The leader or manager might even start to question themselves, wondering what they could have done better or whether *they* are the cause for the employee deciding to leave. Unfortunately, that's a case of "too little too late."

Here's the thing, the reason your employee is going to give you as to why they are leaving is *not going to be the truth*. They will still keep it polite and professional, citing by-the-book reasons. They will be too afraid of burning bridges, and that fear is enough to squash any desire they have to be honest and share the truth. They will not tell you outright that they are leaving because of their tedious work and the demotivation. *They will not tell you that they are leaving because they are not having fun,* although that would have been one of the key points that factored into their decision.

Not having fun at work is a big reason why many companies are *losing good employees*. They are not enjoying themselves because they are not working on projects that challenge and energise them. Every once in a while, we all have to do tasks that we don't necessarily like, even leaders. You might hate talking on the phone, but if your job requires you to speak to a client now and then, it's not the end of the world. However, when an employee finds themselves spending all of their time doing things they hate, the balance is clearly off. This is where leaders run into problems and must quickly think about managing the employee's emotions before they call it quits completely.

The Dreaded Stress Factor

When an employee doesn't love what they do, just the thought of having to go to work is enough to start triggering stress. Globally, feeling stressed in the workplace is on the rise. Employees in China have the highest level of workplace stress, at a staggering 86%, while 91% of Australian adults report that they feel stressed in at least one major area of their lives. 25% of employees say that their job is the number one stress factor in their lives and <u>29%</u> of employees feel quite a bit or extremely stressed when they're at work.

What's worse, job stress is the biggest <u>reason</u> behind why so many employees fall sick, call in sick, and experience financial or personal problems. The dreaded stress factor is unavoidable if your employees are not enjoying themselves. When you love what you do, somehow, everything still feels manageable. Will the stress disappear completely? No, it's still there, but you are not focused on the negative aspects of your job because you love what you do, and that passion for the job is enough to get you through it. It is not uncommon for employees to experience some form of stress-related anxiety or depression in their jobs, an unspoken side effect of what happens when the fun is severely lacking in the environment.

Unfortunately, those types of work conditions are more common than a work environment where leaders understand the importance of ensuring that the employees are enjoying their time at work. A lot of leaders are still stuck in the mindset that fun means work is not getting done, and people are slacking off. They think along the lines of "you're not paid to have fun, you're paid to work," not realising that this attitude and mentality is causing the stress among employees, stress that is counterproductive.

Most people chase success at work, thinking that will make them happy. The truth is that happiness at work will make you successful. —Alexander Kjerulf

Many bosses are so worried about employees having too much fun at work and not performing their duties that they fail to recognise a stressed-out employee *cannot* perform their duties well either. Stress is a genuine problem at work. A recent report indicated that <u>25%</u> of employees feel like screaming out loud when they are at work because of stress. Another <u>14%</u> secretly harboured the desire to punch their colleagues in the face. This is not something you want to experience when you are trying to manage a team of effective, productive employees. Stress is a silent killer, and it becomes worse when we are overworked. Being overworked can affect you significantly, both mentally and physically. We may not feel it while we're working, but when it hits you, it hits hard. One day you wake up and realise that you are completely exhausted and burned out because you've been overworked for far too long.

The environment you spend the most time in is going to have the biggest influence on your psyche. For most people, that's their workplace. If you're constantly in a fast-paced, high-pressured, on-the-go stressful environment, it is likely to be one of your triggers. There is a lot that could be contributing to your stress: a manager that is breathing down your neck over looming deadlines, a heavy workload, or struggling to build bonds and connections with your colleagues. It is hard to think clearly, and employees can feel scattered and forgetful. Every day feels like another day of misery where nothing seems to go right. Do you want your team to feel this way? I hope not. <u>Studies</u> show that those who reportedly undergo a lot of stress feel tired all the time and less productive as their day progresses. These are all genuine consequences of what happens when the fun factor at work is overlooked.

What makes your job as the leader even more challenging when managing a team of diverse employees is that everyone experiences stress very differently. The way one person responds or reacts to the situation probably won't be the same as another person's. One person might struggle when they are under pressure, while another might thrive. This makes it even more difficult to identify when an employee might be feeling too much pressure, even more so since they are unlikely to come to you about it and tell you outrightly, *"I'm feeling stressed at my job."*

Our bodies were not built to cope with too much stress, and once it reaches the chronic stage, it might be too late. The problem is we live in a society that has conditioned us to believe that we need to do more in less time, and poor mental health is the price to be paid. When an employee is feeling stressed at work, they will never be able to live up to their full potential.

May you find the balance of life, time for work but also time for play. Too much of one thing ends up creating stress that no one needs in their life.
—*Catherine Pulsifer*

Having fun at work is no longer an option. *It is a necessity* if you want a team that is performing, motivated, and able to work together as a unit despite the diversity. This way, you will retain your top performers, increase productivity and build overall team strength. It is the leader's role to ensure that your team is engaged and enjoying themselves *without* them having to ask you to do it. Your team is not going to speak up and tell you that they need more fun or that they are feeling stressed. They are not going to speak up because they are not sure if you're going to support them, stigmatise them, or manage them right out of the role, and they are not willing to risk that. Even when you tell them to feel free to come to you with a problem, they are going to be hesitant about it. Your employee *wants* to be at work and do their best, but they can't be at their best if they are not enjoying themselves, plain and simple. Don't wait until it's past the breaking point or for something to happen before you say, *"I should have done this."* By then, it's usually too late. Ensuring that your team is having fun begins from the moment you step into your role as a leader, and it never stops.

The Importance of Having Fun

The human brain has a circuit in the brain that stores and processes emotions involving playfulness. In fact, playing promotes the plasticity of the brain, helping you feel young and happy. It engages the brain's creative areas, something a company can benefit from since creativity leads to better solutions. Most companies are currently making the mistake of separating work from play when what they should be doing is bringing the personal joy of playfulness into the work experience. Are you also guilty of doing this? It may not sound like the conventional image we have of what a work place should look like, but neurologically and emotionally, adding some playfulness is going to be the best approach to take for the sake of your team's long-term happiness.

You have to understand that a group that enjoys having a good time together is *not wasting time*. They are creating a bond without trying too hard, and that relationship is going to carry into the work they have to do together. A team that likes each other performs significantly better than a unit that rubs each other the wrong way or doesn't get along. Having fun as a team builds social and emotional capital, which simultaneously minimises stress and improves their performance at a task.

Herb Kelleher, the former CEO of Southwest Airlines, was a firm believer in using levity to drive productivity. His philosophy was so inspiring that he never had to force anyone to go along with his ideas. He incorporated an element of fun to drive his initiatives, and that is why he is still remembered fondly as a beloved leader. Kelleher once settled a legal suit with an arm-wrestling match, and on several occasions, he used to dress up as Elvis Presley or a rabbit. Why? To keep his employees happy and smiling. Under Kelleher's leadership, Southwest Airlines built a reputation as one of the nation's most profitable airlines, proving that fun at the office is not a waste of time after all.

*Always take **some of the play**, fun, freedom, and wonder of the weekend into your week and your work.*
—Rasheed Ogunlaru

Having fun encourages employees to think outside the box because a team that regularly spends time together will eventually be comfortable enough around each other to let their guards down. When the emotional walls are down and the team is at ease, they are not afraid to speak their mind and bounce ideas back and forth, no matter how impossible or outrageous those ideas may seem. When you establish this level of comfort among the team, that is when they generate some of their best and most innovative ideas and solutions. A work environment that values fun as much as it values hard work is critical in retaining current employees and just as crucial toward attracting new employees. Nobody wants to work for a company that is negative, miserable, and toxic. Fun should not be relegated to the bottom of your priority list. As the leader, you need to be an enabler and allow the fun to thrive in your team.

Permit your employees to be human. Be open to fun and humour at the workplace.

No matter how diverse and different in personality your team may be, if they are enjoying themselves, they will communicate better, and build trust and friendships. When your people are having fun, they are working harder, and managing their stress better. Want to be a great leader and be remembered as a legend the way Kelleher is? Then, fun might be what you need more of in the workplace.

How Do I Tell If My Team Is Enjoying Themselves?

Take a good look at the productivity levels among your team right now. How much work do they get done? Are they meeting the deadlines? Observe their body language when they walk in the door every morning and throughout the day at work. Do they have a smile on their face, stand up tall, make eye contact, look animated, and actively engage in the conversations around them? Or are their shoulders hunched from the invisible burden of stress that they are carrying around with them? Do they look tired, or out of sorts? Do they have a smile that doesn't quite reach their eyes and somehow looks forced?

Communication goes far beyond verbal abilities. Some of the most powerful forms of communication come in the form of body language. While the mouth can tell a lie, body language is far more revealing; what is said in those unspoken and nonverbal cues will show how that person is really feeling. Your team is not going to tell you outrightly that they are unhappy. Even when you ask them, they are going to say everything is alright but their body language is going to tell a different story. Use appraisals or quarterly review sessions as a time to catch up and encourage your employees to be honest with you about what may be weighing on their mind. Make a conscious effort to pay close attention to a person's body language, a skill that is especially useful when conducting face-to-face sessions. Better yet, get the team together to brainstorm how everyone thinks they could be having more fun at work.

Striking a Balance between Work and Play

The idea of having fun at work needs to be redefined. It is not about hanging around in the break room, sipping coffee, talking, and idling your time away. *Having fun at work is about work-life balance*, the friendships you make, not having to stress unnecessarily, and looking forward to coming to work instead of dreading it. That is the definition of having fun at work.

Invest in your work life balance. Time with friends and family is as important as times at work. Getting that out of balance is a path toward unhappiness.

—Stephen Gillett

What does work-life balance look like, and how do you promote it? You could begin to encourage your employees not to take their work home with them. That would be a great place to start. Encourage them to break the habit of bringing work home with them (if that is what they've been doing) and tell them there is *no reason* they should feel guilty about it. You need to remind them that they have already put in 7 to 8 hours of their time during the day to commit to their job, and they should use the rest of the day for themselves.

Another example of how to encourage a more pleasant and enjoyable work environment is to reduce the stress your team feels in terms of work—for example, learning to say "no" when they already have too much on their plate. This is a major one and probably the hardest for most people to do. Saying no can often induce a lot of feelings of guilt, especially when they are worried their job or reputation might be at risk. When talking to your team about a task, tell them, *"I'd like you to take it on, but if it is too much, it's okay if you say no."* Highlight that they shouldn't feel guilty about this and that saying no is an essential time-management skill to prevent them from being perpetually overcommitted and stressed.

When your team feels they have the support of their leader and the ability to say no if they think they are unable to commit to something, they will be a lot happier. Flexibility is an attractive quality to many employees, especially with the modern mindset today that prioritises work-life balance. Additionally, with decreased stress levels, employees are less likely to fall sick. So, let's look at some easy ways to have more fun at work for a better work-life balance.

Celebrating the Little Victories

Too often, a team gets caught up in the bigger goal that you forget to celebrate the little wins and victories along the way. Working toward a big goal is a massive undertaking, and small celebrations in between help remind your team about how far they have come and the remarkable progress they have made working together. This keeps the employees motivated to keep going, and they will be fired up to work much harder to achieve the next milestone. Encourage your team to set their own milestones and decide what the celebration should be to lift their spirits.

Introducing Super Casual Fridays

Ring in the weekend early at work by going beyond the regular "jeans and t-shirt" dress code by taking casual Fridays a step further. Organise team lunches every Friday or end work an hour early so your team can go home and be with their families for the weekend. Don't you lose work progress like this, you ask? In my experience, the last work hour of the week isn't very productive for most employees anyway as they are already thinking about their weekend plans. So, by ending work an hour earlier, you don't lose that much progress, but you gain a lot of positive attribution to the life-side of the scales.

Never get so busy making a living that you forget to make a life. —Dolly Parton

A Little Friendly Competition

A little friendly competition with prizes involved is a great way to lighten the mood around the office. You could organise something mid-week to break the monotony or plan a friendly competition once a month. Get your team to throw out ideas about what they would like the prizes to be, so you are actually giving them something to be excited about.

A Social Network of Your Own

Technology makes almost anything possible, even the ability to create a private social network just for your team. *Yammer* is an example of a service that helps you quickly and easily set up a social network at work. The employees can collaborate, post funny content, and stay up to date on what's happening in their colleagues' lives, like if a special occasion or a birthday is coming up. This increases the emotional bond between your team members, which will impact their motivation positively when working together.

Commit to One Day of "Fun at Work"

The "Fun at Work Day" is one day each month, where the focus is geared toward fun instead of work. Instead of asking your team to give up their weekends to attend team-building retreats, make "Fun at Work Day" happen on a workday. Let it be a day filled with games, team building activities, lunch, and tea-time get together sessions. Some great ideas include allowing your employees to bring their pets to work, take longer lunch breaks, and watch a movie at the office as you bond over food and drinks. Don't think of this as a day of work wasted because the boost of happiness that your employees are going to get out of this one day will more than make up for it. Their productivity levels will soar sky-high when they come into work the next day. It will give them something to work hard for and look forward to every month. I think you will enjoy this day yourself and it is important (even for the leader) to just do nothing once in a while.

I believe a balanced life is essential, and I try to make sure that all of our employees know that and live that way. It's crucial to me as a manager that I help ensure that our employees are as successful as our customers and partners. I also think that employees these days expect less of a separation of work and personal life. That doesn't mean that work tasks should encroach upon our personal time, but it does mean that employees today expect more from the companies for whom they work. [...] The answer for us is to integrate philanthropy with work.
—Marc Benioff

In summary, in order to have more fun at work, you should:

- o Celebrate the little victories
- o Introduce Super Casual Fridays
- o Organise little friendly competitions
- o Create your own social network
- o Commit to one "Fun at Work Day"

CHAPTER 5:

How a Focus on Organisation Will Increase Contribution

First comes thought; then organization of that
thought into ideas and plans; then transformation of
those plans into reality.   —NAPOLEON HILL

a company that is organised will always yield a productive team. Whether it's the team leader or an individual with the capacity to lead, someone must be ensuring that the entire team stays well-ordered. It is the only way to enhance contribution while simultaneously streamlining productivity. If people know where and when to share their valuable insight, they will feel more inclined to do so. There is nowhere that a team thrives better than in an environment where they feel nurtured and supported, in an organised environment with a purpose and a clear, distinct direction.

Organisations need to have a purpose and set goals. But having a goal is one thing, reaching it is another one. That is where being organised comes into play; without a plan of what to do and when to do it, you will never achieve your goals. Organised teams and individuals accomplish more in a day and have it all together. They are the ones who smash through one task after the next until they finally accomplish all that they set out to do, and they do this while making time for themselves, their hobbies, passions, family, and friendships.

When your team is organised, it thrives at what it does, and things get done twice as fast because organised teams don't waste time on unnecessary discussions. They only communicate on the essential points: efficiency, motivation, commitment, and passion. All these elements are what help to shape and mould an organised culture that brings out the best in its people, under excellent leadership, of course.

Being Organised Keeps Your Team Productive

Did you know that the average person will spend <u>one year</u> of their life looking for lost or misplaced items? Imagine the compounding effect of that in an organisation and what would happen if *every member of the team* spent a year of their life looking for misplaced work documents. Organised people very rarely just go with the flow. Instead, they prefer to be organised and plan a list of things that they need to get done for the day, the week, or even the month. It is how they stay on track towards achieving the goals they set for themselves and how they always seem to get more stuff done than those of you who are, say, not as productive as they should be.

If I cannot do great things, I can do small things in a great way. —*Martin Luther King, Jr*

People coming together with the same idea *can make change happen.* They can make a difference. You have to remind your team of this. They are a unit, a community in the office. And if they can learn to harness that collective power and build the consistent habit of staying organised and productive, there is no end to the accomplishments they could achieve. When organised, your people will set goals for themselves. But they are not just setting a goal, they are making a commitment to seeing it through. This commitment is what helps them to stay productive because, in the end, they won't care how long it takes or how hard they have to work, as long as they get the results that they want.

The Time-Saving Factor

When everyone knows what needs to be done, no time is wasted going back and forth with *unnecessary communication about who should be doing what*. As soon as you start the day, you and your team already should have an idea of everything that must be done that day and who should be doing it. Otherwise, you could end up spending too much time talking about delegation and trying to decide how to best distribute your tasks. Every single moment that is not being fully utilised is another moment that is wasted. Every minute and every hour counts, and when you are organised, the time-saving factor is one of the most significant benefits you will gain as a team.

For every minute spent organizing, an hour is earned.
—Benjamin Franklin

Minimal Stress

If a team works well enough and is organised, stress could potentially be eliminated altogether. Not everyone feels productive at the same time. I do my best work in the morning, and maybe for you it is at later times in the day. It doesn't matter when your employees might be feeling that burst of motivation, *as long as the tasks get done* and everyone has done their part. Encourage your team to make the most out of their productivity streak, find the times when they feel the most energetic and productive, and choose that time to make the most of the tasks scheduled. This, however, only works if you are well organised. Otherwise, by the time you reach the end of the day, not everything has been completed, and the entire team starts to get stressed.

Deadlines Acknowledged and Understood

Organisation breeds responsibility; seldom do you find these traits thriving in a person or organisation individually. A team that is organised is one that fully acknowledges and understands deadlines that must be met. There is clarity about what needs to get done, who needs to do it, and when it needs to be finalised. The communication around these deadlines is clear, and every member of the team does their part to make sure these deadlines are met. Why do you think deadlines exist at the workplace? For a simple reason: *because things need to get done.* If your team is organised and productive, it will meet these deadlines without much difficulty resulting in operations progressing smoothly and on schedule, as well as satisfied clients.

Organisation Means Less Clutter

People often spend extra time creating clutter when they feel as though they are not organised. Greg McKeown, author of the bestselling book *Essentialism: The Disciplined Pursuit of Less,* believes that people today are so focused on the concept of "more" that we take on unnecessary things we don't need. This ends up cluttering our lives and eventually making a mess that leads to lower levels of productivity.

Here's the problem with taking on too many things at once. When you underestimate the timeframe needed to complete the tasks you take on, *you end up compromising on a lot of other things*. You compromise on the quality because you are then rushing to meet the deadlines that have been set. You compromise your focus because instead of concentrating on doing one task at a time, it will split your focus on the different tasks. Instead of excelling or achieving success, you are now burned out, worn out, stressed, and still left with the feeling that you could have done better. Clutter is a distraction, and the organised mindset requires that anything which is not useful or contributing productively needs to go.

Our life is frittered away by detail... Simplify, simplify.
—Henry David Thoreau

The Leader *and* the Team Become More Influential

When you are one of the few teams in your company displaying signs of organisation and increased productivity, it is only a matter of time before other employees begin to notice. They will wonder what you and your team are doing right and how you successfully achieve goal after goal. Positive morale at the workplace is essential to keep employees motivated, and other teams and organisations will soon start looking to you for inspiration. They might even ask for your guidance to point them in the right direction. And who doesn't like to be asked for advice?

You Make Money

Ultimately, that is the goal of every business. A company is only as successful as its employees who work for it. When you and your team are disorganised, nothing gets done. When work is neglected, the clients are unhappy. Unhappy clients are not paying clients. But when you are organised, you will all get more done and sometimes even deliver *before* the specified deadline. This means having happy and paying clients, and thus, the business ends up making more money.

Here is a quick summary of the reasons why your team should be organised:

- o You save time
- o Minimal stress
- o Deadlines are acknowledged and understood
- o Less clutter
- o The leader and the team become more influential
- o You make money

One of the best things about being organised and productive is that you can see the efforts your hard work has accomplished. The result of a goal that you have set out to do and then achieved will be hard to ignore. You will feel proud each time you think about what you have accomplished and realise that you did it all by choosing to be more organised and, therefore, more productive.

The Secret Habits of a Highly Organised Team

Every leader wants their team to be successful, but success can mean different things to different people. For me, it's about creating great products or serving customers well. For others, it's about profitable growth. No matter what your team's definition of success is, it is the leader's responsibility to set the right things in motion so the desired result can be achieved. You could have all the best strategies up your sleeve, but your ability to execute your strategy and reach your goal depends on your team and how organised they are.

A well-structured team also needs a leader who is as organised in the first place. There is nothing worse than a leader who is scattered and all over the place. Remember that everyone is looking to you for guidance, even if they are working remotely. It is you that they take their orders from. An effective leader is clear on the organisation's goals and what needs to be achieved. There are certain habits that highly organised individuals, leaders, and teams live by. And they are a huge reason why these teams and individuals are successful.

They Are Proactive

Success and innovation don't just happen on their own. You need to *make them happen.* Everyone knows what they are supposed to do and why their role matters, but they also need to act accordingly. When all you see is clutter surrounding your life, you can't help but feel hopeless sometimes, wondering how it came to this. These feelings will be amplified over time if nothing is done about the mental and physical disorder around you (in terms of projects and paperwork that keep piling up). As the cluster grows, your feelings of misery and despair may become worse. So, how do you prevent this from happening? By being proactive. Being proactive averts this stress because you actually get your work done before it starts piling up.

The only way to get a thing done is to start to do it.
—Langston Hughes

They Give Themselves a Daily Goal

Daily goals are the easiest way to beat procrastination. When it is clear what work needs to be done at the end of the day, you know exactly what you have to do, and there is *no excuse for not working* on these tasks. Breaking your big goals into smaller chunks also makes it easier to see progress and build momentum. Instead of standing in front of a massive goal, you are now working on manageable exciting tasks and getting closer to reaching your larger goals every single day. Every team member needs to set a daily goal, even if the task at hand may be something small. Training themselves to wake up each day with a goal and the intention to get things done helps them get into the organised mindset and way of thinking.

They Create a System That Works

Productive people never want to lose all the hard work they have done so far, and so an organised team understands how important it is to always have a system that works. I am not talking about how the company is structured or how the business plan is set up to reach a goal (although these are crucial as well). What I mean is a system where all the information is stored in a shared database, readily accessible at any time. *Keeping your files safe and secure* is not a problem anymore with the myriad of tools available. Saving documents and backing up your data digitally is the greener way to go. Successful and organised leaders understand this, and that is why you need to store information in a system that you trust and encourage your team to do the same. Apps like *OneNote*, *Google Drive*, and *Evernote* that have accessible servers across the world keep your data safely backed up. Storing information digitally also makes it much easier to share information with every member of the team quickly and easily, with the added bonus of being able to access the information anytime and anywhere you need it.

> *A good system shortens the road to the goal.*
> —*Orison Swett Marden*

They Don't Let Distractions Get to Them

Distractions are everywhere, but organised people have mastered the art of blocking them out and not letting them bother them. If you want to *be productive*, you will have to do the same and remove all causes for temptation when you need to buckle down and get something done.

Start with cleaning up your working place. Get rid of all the clutter on your desk that could take away your attention from the task you are working on. The same goes for digital distractions; close unnecessary tabs and put your phone in airplane mode and somewhere you can't see it. Also, try to create as much silence in your work environment as possible. If you are working at home, find a quiet place and let everyone know that you don't want to be disturbed while working. In an office, throw on headphones and play some white noise or calm, lyric-free music to maximise your concentration. It is essential to remove as many distractions as possible, especially if there is an important task you need to attend to.

They Always Have a Backup

I've got a quick rule of thumb for you: if running out of something is going to cause an interruption in your life, make it a practice to keep backups of critical items where feasible. Organised people and teams always have a backup of the essential items they need to stay productive, so if they ever run out of something, they've still got a spare on hand that is ready to use, and *no precious time gets wasted* in the process. For machines and other expensive material, I recommend you to rent or borrow the items from a neighbouring organisation (business, school, government agency) rather than buying in duplicate.

They Eliminate Bad Habits

For positive change to happen, habits need to change first. How could you aim to have a new, organised way of working as a team if you still stick to your former bad habits? Encourage your team to get rid of old thought patterns that made them feel stressed, unproductive, and demotivated in the past and replace them with thoughts that will surge them forward on the path to success. What you're trying to do now is break the cycle, which means ditching all those bad habits that once stopped the team from reaching its full potential. Set rules to help you make decisions and commit to them.

Old ways may feel comfortable, but they may not be the most effective.

Clutter is not just physical stuff. It's old ideas, toxic relationships and bad habits. Clutter is anything that does not support your better self. —Eleanor Brown

They Manage Their Expectations Wisely

Disappointments and rejection can be too much for some people to handle, especially if they seem to happen a lot. When it looks like you are facing more rejection than you can manage, it can be off-putting, and that is when confidence begins to fade away. An organised team manages their expectations to *minimise disappointments*. They fully understand what they need to do and what the realistic outcomes might be. Setting unrealistic expectations is just another way of purposely setting yourself up for failure. But when your employees know what to expect, they are less likely to feel demotivated and give up.

They Live by Their To-Do Lists

Organised people are never without a to-do list. There may be a lot to do, but the key to doing it all is to pace yourself right from the start. The sluggishness as the day progresses can be the biggest challenge to overcome, and it is going to be even harder to do if you don't get things organised with a to-do list. Long-distance runners don't exhaust all their energy supply as soon as they leave the starting line. They start at a steady pace and maintain that momentum, so it is enough to sustain them until the finish line. Encourage every team member to create a collective and personal to-do list of everything that needs to get done for the day. *Start the morning with the most demanding tasks and slowly work your way down the list*. Without a to-do list, before you know it, half the day is gone, and you would have barely made a dent in your tasks.

It takes as much energy to wish as it does to plan.
—*Eleanor Roosevelt*

Values Are Practiced Throughout the Team

This helps to foster an environment of trust within the team. Values like honesty and respect hold people accountable, and the team is able to *bond over the values* that they have set together as a team. Being aligned and practising the same values foster a sense of unity, and knowing that you can depend on each other to get the job done is a great feeling. I have pinned my list of the most important team values in the cafeteria of my office. Due to this, every time an employee or manager enters the room to take a break, they are reminded of those values (you can download this list at the beginning and the end of the book).

They Focus on Efficiency Rather Than Excuses

A motivated and organised team finds ways to increase their productivity by minimising the time spent working on activities individually when they can be grouped together. That is where the to-do list comes in handy. Viewing the list of items written down, it is easy to see which similar tasks can be grouped and worked on simultaneously, so you *don't double your workload by going back and forth*. Organised people don't make excuses for why they couldn't get something done because they hold themselves accountable. It is easy to put off unpleasant tasks, but that is just an excuse to procrastinate. If there is no concrete reason why you shouldn't start something, then don't look for excuses not to do it.

If you want to make an easy job seem mighty hard, just keep putting off doing it. —Olin Miller

To recapitulate, these are the habits you and your team need to pick up if you want to become more organised:

o   Be proactive
o   Give yourself a daily goal
o   Create a system that works
o   Don't let distractions get to you
o   Always have a backup
o   Eliminate bad habits
o   Manage your expectations
o   Live by your to-do lists
o   Practice values throughout the team
o   Focus on efficiency rather than excuses

Oh, Don't Forget About Self-Discipline

A lack of self-discipline among your team can turn into a major setback. Your team may have the intention to achieve great things. They may have the aim to be highly successful. They may have the intent to meet all their deadlines and more. The problem is, they might be struggling with the self-discipline aspect of it, which only further highlights the need for organisation and purpose. If your team does not have a system, and they are flitting from day to day with no real purpose or goal in mind to work towards, they won't be achieving anything of real significance. They will have no idea how to get to where they want to be. To get your mind focused on heading in the right direction, it needs a distinctive driving force that will continuously push it to keep going and not stop until the finish line has been reached. And what is that magic force? Self-discipline.

Self-discipline is about your mindset. It is about how your brain has been programmed to work, and that is something many teams struggle with today. A great example of weak self-discipline is the pursuit of instant gratification. This is the reason why so many have fallen off the road to success. It starts with scrolling through social media and getting these quick dopamine rushes instead of beginning the work you should actually be doing. The thought of having access to instant gratification, instead of sacrificing and waiting for that pleasure to present itself in the future, is a thought that not many are able to resist. Resisting social media, the desire to get a coffee, or even a quick chat with a co-worker, will not be possible if we don't have the self-discipline needed to help us along the way.

If overwhelming goals is something that your team is struggling with, help them cope by encouraging them to create a shift in their mindset. Remind them that nothing worth having is ever going to come easy or be handed to them on a silver platter. Without the challenge and stress of failure, we wouldn't have the chance to grow. In my opinion, learning to embrace this discomfort as part of the journey is how you stay motivated and disciplined enough to keep putting one foot in front of the other. Each time your employees embrace discomfort, they are working on building and strengthening that self-discipline mental muscle.

Out of clutter, find simplicity. From discord, find harmony. In the middle of difficulty lies opportunity.
—Albert Einstein

Better yet, encourage your team to embrace persistence too. Persistence can be a surprisingly rewarding emotion because each time you force yourself to see a task through, the result will make you feel much happier and better about yourself. As part of this ripple effect, that feeling will drive you to want to do more and see just how far you can go if you only just persist on a task. Persistence makes victories that much more valuable. If success always came easy, we would never appreciate it as much.

Step III:
Improve Your and Your
Team's Communication

CHAPTER 6:

The Secrets of EQ and Vulnerability

Let's not forget that the little emotions are the great captains of our lives and we obey them without realizing it. —VINCENT VAN GOGH

E mbracing diversity, encouraging fun, motivation, happiness, and productivity—there are so many aspects of successfully leading a team. Having your attention pulled in different directions makes it easy to forget to focus on the finer subtleties. One such finer nuance is the emotional intelligence (EQ) aspect. We are all highly emotional creatures by nature, and over the last few years, the importance of emotional intelligence has been brought to the forefront. We should recognise and understand the importance of having the freedom to be openly expressive with our emotions.

A powerful team consists of individuals with a heightened focus upon their emotional intelligence and those who are willing to communicate with one another, even in the most vulnerable of times. In my experience, this open line of communication has been immensely helpful in encouraging better work flow among a diverse team and empowering confidence in each member to speak their mind. Emotional intelligence is the next secret ingredient you need to remove resistance and generate a positive team culture that can bring productive change.

Most people are afraid to talk about their emotions. Society has conditioned us to believe that showing emotions is a sign of weakness—a lack of control. We are taught to keep our chin up and have a stiff upper lip, presenting a strong facade even though that is far from what we may be feeling on the inside. This negative connotation associated with emotions is the reason why emotional intelligence was never given much focus in the past until now.

What Does It Mean to Be Emotionally Intelligent?

It is crucial to distinguish the difference between emotions and the value that *emotional intelligence* has. Emotional intelligence, commonly referred to as EQ, is the ability to identify and manage *your emotions* and the emotions of *others.* It is possible to increase your EQ, so let's take a deeper look at it.

EQ requires emotional awareness, and having empathy towards yourself as well as others. It also calls for the ability to harness your emotions and apply them to tasks like thinking or problem-solving. It requires the ability to manage emotions, which includes regulating your own feelings and the emotions of the people around you. If someone needs to be calmed down, the EQ leader (= a leader with high EQ) knows what to do and how to do it effectively. If someone needs cheering up, the EQ leader is able to make them feel better. Emotions are responsible for some of the best and worst moments in our lives. Emotions are the reason why love feels so incredible, yet they are also the reason why breakups feel so terrible. They are the reason why getting a promotion at work makes you feel jubilant, and at the same time, they are responsible for the misery and unhappiness you feel after losing your job.

We define emotional intelligence as the subset of social intelligence that involves the ability to monitor one's own and others' feelings and emotions, to discriminate among them and to use this information to guide one's thinking and actions. —Salovey and Mayer

Are you an emotional person? It does not matter because being very emotional doesn't automatically mean you have a high level of EQ. You may be displaying your emotions freely*; but that does not mean that you are thinking about your emotions or why you have them.* That's the difference. You might not even be considering the appropriateness of showing these emotions in certain situations. The problem is that we are not taught the value of emotions growing up. If your family members didn't understand the importance of EQ or practiced it themselves, then chances are you were probably not exposed to this either. Children and teenagers often struggle to contain their emotions, and emotions hit them hard because they can neither fully understand their feelings or those of others.

People judge, bully each other, get stuck in toxic friendships and relationships, and hurt each other. Why? All due to insecurity and a lack of emotional intelligence. It is hard to differentiate between yourself and someone else, and it is even more challenging to connect on an emotional level. To change that and truly comprehend where someone else is coming from, we have to consider emotional intelligence as a significant skill in our society. We must take the time to work on it consciously. Unfortunately, most leaders do neither.

The Difference Between EQ and IQ

If you're already familiar with emotional intelligence, you have probably heard about Daniel Goleman (author of the bestselling book *Emotional Intelligence*) and his concepts which are linked closely to leadership abilities. He states that EQ is focused on how smart you are in the way that you interact with your own emotions and with other people. It is not merely about communicating with the people around you, but how effectively you interact with them.

IQ, on the other hand, is more about pattern recognition, reasoning and logical problem-solving. At work, you can see first-hand why the importance of EQ over IQ is apparent. Although IQ is certainly one of the main ingredients towards achieving success, EQ is a trait that many businesses will look for in a potential leader first. This is because a leader's primary job would be to lead the people around them. They need to inspire others, to get their teams working well together in a cohesive and unified manner, and to manage conflict when it arises. All of these skills require that the leader is able to gauge emotions and read the people around them. It is EQ that helps leaders distinguish and identify what an employee's strengths and weaknesses are, not IQ. It is EQ that will enable leaders to get along well with various groups of individuals, not IQ. To possess great social skills and excel with the clients, you need a high EQ, not IQ.

Comparing the three domains, I found that for jobs of all kinds, emotional competencies were twice as prevalent among distinguishing competencies as were technical skills and purely cognitive abilities combined. In general, the higher a position in an organization, the more EI [emotional intelligence] mattered: for individuals in leadership positions, 85 percent of their competencies were in the EI domain. —Daniel Goleman

Do We Need Emotions in a Team?

Yes, we do, unless you want to work with robots. Emotions help us understand the people around us based on the way we express ourselves through facial expression and body language. They are clues that help us understand how a person is feeling and what our next actions should be.

Social communication is a big part of how we develop meaningful relationships, and as a leader, it is a crucial step in the process. The way you act has a profound influence on the group. A charismatic leader can inspire great change and have a positive effect on the people. Ultimately, teamwork is more efficient and flourishes when we understand that empathy can go a long way. Our emotions construct a big part of who we are. We may try to hide them, ignore them, live in denial about them, but emotions are essentially what makes us so wonderfully, beautifully human.

Emotions are the glue that holds the cells of the organism together. —Candace Pert

Why has emotional intelligence become a necessity in today's world? Because you are more likely to fall into negative behaviour patterns when you don't have a high EQ guiding the way. A prime example would be a time when you handled a situation poorly, and it ended up costing you a great deal. You regret how you managed things at the time, and if you could turn back the clock, you would do it so much better. Dwelling on this negative experience only makes matters worse. You will become more frustrated and pessimistic with your life. You can sometimes see the effects of what happens when people don't know what to do with their emotions; they become anxious, depressed, demoralised, withdrawn, anti-social, problematic, have numerous social problems, and more. I don't think that is the path you would like to take, so understand your emotions and learn how to react to them.

The Emotionally Intelligent Leader

EQ is a skill that needs to be learned, and like every other new skill you set out to learn, it starts with understanding which areas you need to improve on. You want to be able to master them to a point where you are no longer actively thinking about it; you just do it like driving a car. And like learning how to drive, EQ needs practice, *a lot* of practice. Everything is difficult before it gets easy. In the beginning, it is difficult because you will have to put in conscious effort in thinking about it all the time and expending all your mental energy to focus on getting it right, but after a while, it will come automatically and be less demanding.

Leading a team without understanding its emotions is like driving a car without knowing how to change gears (and no, it's not an automatic one). In the past, the leader would decide the direction. All the people were simply following his or her lead. All teams were following in the leader's footsteps. Leadership is no longer like that. It is now about creating connections and creating relationships, so you need to be able to manage emotions in this new kind of environment. To become the emotionally intelligent leader capable of leading your team to great success, multiple things must be done.

Acknowledge Emotions

Antonio Damasio's <u>research</u> revealed that those who had experienced damage in the part of the brain that dealt with emotions found themselves having a much harder time making rational decisions. Damasio talked about his patient named Elliot, who had a brain tumour removed, along with a part of the frontal lobe that had been affected. After the surgery, Elliot experienced a shift in his decision-making abilities. His ability to plan for the future and make decisions seemed to have weakened. Damasio wrote in his words: *"Elliot appears to be a man with normal intellect who was unable to decide properly, especially when the decisions involved personal or social matters."* We make decisions based on our feelings; that is how important emotions are to us. This is why you need to acknowledge your and others' emotions so you understand the decision-making process in every situation.

Acknowledging emotions is the first small step you can take to improve your EQ. Instead of denying them, try observing them with a curious mind. Ask people with genuine interest how they are feeling. When *you* are asked about how you are feeling, answer with authenticity. Additionally, don't forget to tell your team to do the same. Instead of complaining about their colleagues behind their back, encourage them to talk about the way they feel.

> *When awareness is brought to an emotion, power is brought to your life.* —Tara Meyer Robson

Erase the Taboo

When your team talks about or reveals their emotions, tell them it is okay to do so. Reassure them that emotions are not something to feel guilty about, but rather something that can be learned from. Instead of being afraid to address emotions, *embrace talking about them openly*. You can set an example by erasing the taboo that exists in our society when it comes to talking about emotions because this taboo is what's stopping all of us from taking the next step.

Reflect on the Origin of That Emotion

Remember the last time you got really upset or anxious. How did it feel? Why were you feeling this way? How can you prevent this from happening again? Knowing why we experience a particular emotion helps us deal with and process our feelings. It gives us time to actively reflect on how these emotions make us feel mentally and physically. It also gives us time to think about what triggered the emotion, and with these details, we can think about how to handle specific situations better, moving forward.

Analysing and Accepting Emotions

Every emotion has a different way it should be handled, and therefore, it is important to get to the root cause of the feeling. Accept and appreciate all those emotions because they are neither good nor bad. It is *the way that we handle them* that makes a difference. Why are we so desperately trying to cut grievance and sadness out of our lives? To pretend we are okay rather than embrace how we feel? In truth, grief and sadness can be a beautiful illustration of our appreciation for someone or something.

We cannot tell what may happen to us in the strange medley of life. But we can decide what happens in us — how we can take it, what we do with it — and that is what really counts in the end.   —Joseph Fort Newton

Ask Your Team Questions

Ask your team, *"How do you feel about...?"*. As a leader, you cannot manage a team's energy if you don't know how they think about goals, new challenges, their team, or new colleagues at work. It is crucial to ask your employees for their opinion so that you can adjust the necessary things and improve the work environment.

Learning to Listen Better

Learn how to be present in a conversation and how to share your feelings when you talk to your team. People have great ideas, and if you take the time to listen and let them get their point across, you are *demonstrating respect* for their opinions. This, in turn, makes them feel comfortable about opening up to you, which then allows you to regulate their emotions effectively. This use of emotional intelligence eventually leads to better teamwork and increased productivity all around.

Emotional intelligence is the ability to sense, understand, and effectively apply the power and acumen of emotions as a source of human energy, information, connection, and influence.   —Robert K. Cooper, Ph.D.

To summarise, this is what you must do to become an emotionally intelligent leader:

o   Acknowledge emotions
o   Erase the taboo
o   Reflect on the origin of emotions
o   Analyse and accept emotions
o   Ask your team questions
o   Learn to listen better

As soon as you master your emotions, and in the process, get better at it, you will find it easier and easier to handle the emotions of others. Becoming an emotionally intelligent leader is a journey that begins by simply asking a person how you can support them. If we were all emotionally intelligent, what a difference would it make in the way we address variation? How would we approach topics like mental health? Imagine the world that we would be living in; an environment full of mutual understanding, acceptance, tolerance, and connection—a truly inclusive world. Now, wouldn't that be something?

Building Your Emotionally Intelligent Team

As an effective leader, you should use your EQ skills to influence and persuade others under your leadership to pursue and work together towards a common goal. In an organisation, productivity levels run higher when a leader with a high EQ is present. These leaders are the driving force behind the collective success of a group. It is always a group effort, but the one who inspires the achievement behind the scenes is the EQ leader. How can you do this? By building an emotionally intelligent team.

Vanessa Urch Druskat and Steven B. Wolff, the people behind *Building the Emotional Intelligence of Groups* research findings, affirm that emotional intelligence skills are the underlying principle upon which successful teams are effectively built. EQ makes you (and every employee) a better team player with a greater capacity to genuinely connect on a deep and meaningful level with the team. Hard conversations become easier when empathy, self-awareness, and social skills are present. It also improves your situational awareness, which means that you are in tune and present, always aware of what is happening as it unfolds.

In a study of skills that distinguish star performers in every field from entry-level jobs to executive positions, the single most important factor was not IQ, advanced degrees, or technical experience, it was EQ. Of the competencies required for excellence in performance in the job studies, 67% were emotional competencies.
—Daniel Goleman

EQ gives you control over your thought process too. The way you form your thinking directly impacts the emotions that you feel. If you were already feeling angry, for example, allowing your mind to run free with thoughts that feed into your anger will only make matters worse. It requires a lot of self-control, but the best way of regulating your emotions is to exercise some control over your thoughts. Controlling what you allow yourself to think will make it easier for you to dissociate and remove yourself from the overpowering force of negative and unpleasant emotions. When you can remove yourself from the equation, making rational and more objective decisions becomes much easier.

The best way to start controlling your thoughts is by meditating. You have probably heard this a thousand times, but I can assure you that it helps. Every morning I sit down, focus only on my breath and do nothing else for ten minutes. That is all it takes (but it is harder than you would expect). I recommend you start meditating, and you will notice how your awareness of all the thoughts running through your head will improve significantly.

Setting the Team Norms

As the leader, you get the opportunity to set the norms for your team. Start based on the following Druskat and Wolff philosophy:

"It's not always about having team members who are working through the night trying to meet deadlines. It's about THANKING them for doing it. It's not about discussing ideas in depth. It's about asking the quiet member of the group what they think. It's about acknowledging when there is unexpressed tension, false harmony, and treating everyone with respect."

Moving forward, this should be the new norm that every team member is encouraged to follow.

Encourage Relationships with Other Teams

Employees who work and play together stay together as a team. Bonding with colleagues encourages *interpersonal relationships* not only with each other but also with other teams within the organisation. If you organise lunches, meetings, and friendly get-togethers with other departments regularly, everyone gets the opportunity to get to know each other. Not only will your employees have fun making new friends, but their emotional intelligence will also improve with every new social experience.

Promote Team Respect and Understanding

Have you ever found yourself wanting to have a conversation with someone, but they were looking at their phone the whole time? Encourage your team to put their phone, tablet, or papers away and show mutual respect by prioritising face-to-face interactions. Treat everyone in the office with respect, trust, and appreciation. Be courteous, compassionate, and caring, encouraging your team *to treat each other the way they would like to be treated*, and promote a sense of empathy.

Supplying the Right Resources

If you want your team to learn about emotional intelligence, then you need to ensure all the resources are on hand for them to learn about it. Talk about EQ often with your employees, show them useful books and podcasts. This way, the topic of emotional intelligence becomes a norm among your team, and the employees are more likely to inform themselves and get better at it.

Emotional competence is the single most important personal quality that each of us must develop and access to experience a breakthrough. Only through managing our emotions can we access our intellect and our technical competence. An emotionally competent person performs better under pressure. —Dave Lennick

Inter-Departmental Understanding

A core EQ skill is empathy and the ability to walk a mile in another's shoes to *understand what they have to go through* on a daily basis. Give your team the opportunity to learn about how the other groups in the organisation work and what their strategies are. That way, the next time they need to collaborate on a project, they are fully aware of what the other party needs to deal with instead of just focusing on the self-interest of their team alone.

In short, to build your emotionally intelligent team, you must:

- o Set the team norms
- o Encourage relationships with other teams
- o Promote team respect and understanding
- o Supply the right resources
- o Establish an inter-departmental understanding

Don't Be Afraid to Be Vulnerable

Vulnerability is an emotion that is often feared. It is about risk. Vulnerability is about uncertainty. It is defined as the possibility of being harmed or attacked, either emotionally or physically. Being vulnerable is a terrifying prospect for some. The very idea of leaving themselves open to the possibility of being hurt is enough for them to put their guard up and build emotional walls around themselves. This is an attempt to protect themselves, and it is perfectly understandable. Nobody wants to be hurt. Nobody wants to be taken advantage of. Not everyone experiences vulnerability, but when they do, they are *afraid* of letting it show. Even more so if they happen to be in a position of power, like a leader.

Putting on a brave face all the time can be exhausting, both mentally and physically. Somewhere along the way, you develop the belief that if you show your weak side, people might take advantage of it or, worse, you open yourself up to being hurt. But that is *not true at all*. On the contrary, being open to the idea of letting your vulnerability show can be *liberating*. Show your vulnerable side because as terrifying and scary as it is, you need to know that you can count on some of the relationships you have, especially at time you need them the most.

Vulnerability is the core, the heart, the centre of meaningful human experiences. —Brene Brown

A vulnerable leader is someone that people admire. It takes tremendous amounts of courage to be vulnerable, and emotional intelligence will give you this courage. People appreciate authenticity, and they respect you even more when you are 100% genuine with them instead of trying to be something that you are not. When you can fully admit you don't have all the answers, that you don't know what to do at times, and that you are just as worried about failure as they are, they will admire your courage and place you in a leadership position almost naturally. But being comfortable with the idea of being vulnerable takes practice. Take it slow, and maybe once a week, sit down with your team and talk about one weakness that you would normally try to hide. Tell them how you feel, why you feel that way. Ask them if anyone else feels the same and talk about how everyone could support each other better moving forward. Practicing vulnerability is a simple step of being honest and talking about your "weaknesses."

Step IV:
Set Your Team Free

CHAPTER 7:
Why You Need to Let Go

You may be deceived if you trust too much, but you will live in torment if you don't trust enough.

—FRANK CRANE

*Y*ou are now at the final stage of achieving top teamwork at your workplace. You have laid the groundwork and taken all the steps that you need to set your team up for success. Now, this last leg is just as crucial as all the other steps you've learned so far. Once you have done everything you can as a leader, you need to *trust your team and set them free*. Yes, this means a complete release of any attempts at control and absolute trust in their abilities to get the job done. Each team member has been given their position because they are the best fit to conduct those actions, and this should be sufficient to allow them to do those things on their own. Do not micromanage in any way, or you will lose your team's trust and coherence. They will crumble if you insist on telling them exactly how to do their job. Remember this; great leaders don't micromanage or control, they *lead*.

You've given the members their vision and their purpose. You've given them a goal, and you've encouraged them to embrace their differences and work together as a team. You've given them all that they need to coral around a joint mission and band together to overcome the odds as a team. You, being their leader, now need to tap into the most powerful emotional tool you can tap into: *trust*.

The Value of Trust

If your team feels like you trust them, they will be more willing to put their neck out for you and go the extra mile. Trust and respect go a long way in successful and effective leadership. It is the most important thing in human relations. Without trust, there is no possibility of working well together. For a leader to be considered successful, they would always need to cultivate an environment of trust with their team. A team should trust each other and know, without a doubt, that they can put their full confidence in their leader to always have their best interest at heart. This is what makes a happier, more positive team all around. When there's trust, greater and more effective work relationships between the leader, team members, and colleagues can exist. This paves the way for collaboration as each member believes that they work well together as a team. Trust your employees to get the job done, and they will. Trust them, and they will trust you in return.

Few things help an individual more than to place responsibility upon him, and to let him know that you trust him. —Booker T. Washington

What does a trusting team look like? Let's look at an example. The Four Seasons Hotel in Las Vegas is a beautiful hotel. The reason for that is not the fancy beds or the extravagant decor; any hotel can buy an elegant bed and have brilliantly decorated rooms. No, the reason it is a beautiful hotel is because of the people who work there. When you walk through the halls of the hotel, you get a distinct feeling that the people working in the hotel said "hello," not because they *had to* say "hello" as part of their jobs. It is because they *wanted* to say "hello." That is the difference, and we are more attuned to the emotions of others than we realise. We can tell the difference between forced great customer service and genuinely excellent customer service. When the person serving you is being funny and engaging and loves what they do, you can tell in the service they provide. It shows in their beaming smile and helpful personality.

As a leader or manager, you can do one of two things when you walk past your employees throughout the workday. The first is, you can ask the employees how they are doing, trusting that they are carrying out their responsibilities. Second, you can walk past your employees, checking on work without acknowledging the employee's feelings or needs. Which leadership approach do you think works best? The answer is the first one because, with that leadership style, you are allowing your employees to *feel* like they can do their best. The first approach is going to provide your customers with a profoundly different experience than the second one. Not because of the employee, but because of the *leaders*.

It is the leaders who are responsible for creating an environment where the employee feels like they can be themselves. A disgruntled employee will already be going through a range of emotions. And this will show in the kind of work they produce and the service they provide to the customers. Leaders often ask, *"How do I get the most out of my team?"*. But your team is not a used, wet towel; you are not trying to wring as much as you possibly can out of it before you toss it in the laundry. They are people with feelings. The right question to ask instead is:

"How do I create an environment where my team can work at their best naturally?"

The answer is trust. That is how you produce an environment where your team feels safe enough to step forward and say, *"I'm sorry, I've made a mistake."* Because mistakes happen, they are a part of how we learn on the job and get better. Tell them to see mistakes as an experience to learn and think about what they would do differently should they face such a situation again. It isn't going to help anyone to be overly critical each time there is a slip or a wrong move made. Your employee is probably beating themselves up enough already and anxious about the mistake they have made. They are feeling stressed and worried about it, and the last thing you should do is make them feel even worse. That is not the way to build trusting teams.

Trust your team enough to be accountable for what they are doing and responsible enough to raise their hands and say, *"I'm not sure what I'm doing. I need help."* They must be comfortable enough to speak up without fear of retribution. Would you admit you need support if it put your job at risk? No? That's what I thought. Your employees need to believe that when they ask for help, their team and their leaders will come running to their aid. That is what a trusting team should be. That is what a team on its way to achieving success looks like. Most employees can't tell you what they even *think* good leadership looks like, but they can immediately tell you what bad leadership *feels like*. You don't want to be the latter.

The glue that holds all relationships together — including the relationship between the leader and the led — is trust.
—Brian Tracy

When trust among a team does not exist, then all you are left with is a group of secretly unhappy people who are coming to work each day, faking and lying their way through just to cash a paycheck at the end of the month. If trust among a team does not exist, your team is certainly not going to tell you when they've made a mistake or when they need help with what they are doing. Your team will hoard the information they have, keeping it to themselves for fear that someone else might get the glory for their ideas. Without trust, that is going to be the team culture, and over time, your team will crumble. It is inevitable.

You have probably experienced firsthand what lousy customer service feels like, but most of us never stop to ask *why* the employee is reacting that way. Why does the employee fake a smile? Why do we feel like we are on the receiving end of the employee's frustration? Why does the employee treat us like nothing more than just another paying customer they can't wait to be done with instead of treating each other like fellow human beings? If you stopped to ask them, the answer you would probably get in return would sound something like *if they don't do what they are told and follow the rules, they could lose their jobs.* That is all you need to know. That kind of fear among employees means they are not secure in their careers. They are not happy in their profession, and their managers or leaders don't trust them enough to do the job they have been trained and hired to do. That is what happens when trust is lacking in a team and its leader. The employee becomes more focused on protecting themselves from getting into trouble with their company instead of providing a great experience for the paying customer and doing their job well.

There is a reason why people love flying with Herb Kelleher's Southwest Airlines, and it's not because the company has a magic formula or somehow got lucky and hired all the best people they could find. It is because the people who work there feel safe enough in their own team (you'd probably feel safe expressing yourself too if your boss came to work dressed like a rabbit). Learn to leave your employees alone once you've given them a task to work on, but make sure you are always around just in case they need help.

How to Build Trust in the Workplace

Your team needs to trust that they can come to you for advice and help. Sometimes, this could include complaints or concerns that are personal and may not be related to work at all. It might seem like no big deal to you, but to your employee, their complaints are a very big deal indeed. Work is not always going to be a smooth ride, and there will be challenges along the way. Sometimes, the employee just wants someone who listens to them. They want to know that their opinions and their feelings matter. They make an effort to come into work each day and give it their best, and in return, they just want to know that they are important to the management. As a leader, you can make them feel better by simply acknowledging their concerns and empathising with what they might be going through.

People follow leaders by choice. Without trust, at best you get compliance. —Jesse Lyn Stoner

Be supportive of your employees in any way. There may be times when listening alone is all they need. At other times, offering a solution is the support your employee is looking for. Actively listening is important here since it gives you an idea about what they might need. If a sincere apology is in order, don't hesitate to give it. A simple *"I'm sorry for your situation"* or *"I'm sorry you had to deal with that, let me see what I can do to help"* can do wonders to appease your employee's emotions. It lets your employee know that you are sincerely sorry about the inconvenience they may have experienced, and this attempt at understanding them will not go unnoticed.

Encourage your team to come to you whenever they have a problem and when they do, *thank them for it.* If you think about it, the employee trusted you enough to come to you with their complaints, hoping for a solution, and you should thank them for that trust to let them know you appreciate it. Not only will they be taken by surprise, but you would also have successfully appeased an otherwise frustrated employee with those two simple words alone.

Discourage Gossip

Trust cannot exist if one person is always worried that others in the group are talking about them behind their back. Office gossip and worrying about whether you can fully trust your co-worker is an additional and *unnecessary distraction*. Working with so many different personalities means there is bound to be a clash of some sort. You are not going to get along with everybody, and not everyone is going to like you.

But when you work in a team, you must be able to trust each other if that dynamic is ever going to work. Set the example by discouraging office gossip and not partaking in it yourself. When you hear gossip floating around, find its source and let the whole team know that you are shutting it down. Let them know that they can come to you if there is something they need to get off their chest, but refraining from the gossip about each other is a norm for the team, and you expect them to respect that.

Be Consistent in Your Approach

Do you know someone who one day behaves one way but completely different the next day? It is impossible to trust someone like that as you don't really know what to do or what to think about them. To be effective, you must be consistent in the way you do things; be consistent in your treatment and your rewards, in your methods of leadership, and in your principles. For example, schedule consistent catch-up sessions where everyone has to give their input. Stick to the rules you have set and treat every team member the same. If the employees notice you are inconsistent in your approach, they will lose trust in you. And *when mistrust comes in, love goes out.*

Keep an Open Mind

Listen with an open mind, and you will be much more receptive to what you're hearing. If your team feels like you are willing to give, receive and listen to criticisms with an open mind, in the long run, it will benefit everyone (both the leader and the team). When you know what your weaknesses are, you can work on improving them. And that is what being successful is all about.

Trust is not simply a matter of truthfulness, or even constancy. It is also a matter of amity and goodwill. We trust those who have our best interests at heart, and mistrust those who seem deaf to our concerns.
—Gary Hamel

Praise Them Genuinely

Learn to care about the people on your team genuinely. The best leaders have a high consideration factor, and they care about their people. It is not enough to compliment your employees when they have achieved a goal. If the praise is not genuine, they will see straight through it. Before you can get to the point where your team feels appreciated, you must start to *genuinely* appreciate them. If you can learn to get to that point, your employees are going to notice. Once they see how you really care about the way they feel and that you don't want anyone to feel hurt by another's actions, they will eventually learn to follow in your footsteps.

Invest in Their Development

If you want to keep your team together, it is critical to invest in their development. People want to work in a company where they are empowered to learn, grow, and develop their skills—an environment where they can *explore their full potential.* When your team feels like you are invested in them because you trust them, they will become more engaged and be motivated to work even harder so as not to let you down. Investing in their development shows your team that you favour promoting from within. And it shows that you will reward those who have put in the hard work. It is a sign that you recognise and appreciate all they have to offer, and you are willing to invest in that to see how much further they can go. Investing in your people is going to be one of the smartest leadership decisions you can make.

In summary, you will build trust in the workplace when you:

- o Discourage gossip
- o Be consistent in your approach
- o Keep an open mind
- o Praise your employees genuinely
- o Invest in your team's development

Don't Be a Micromanaging Nightmare

One of the best things you can do as a leader is to let your people do things the way they want. As long as the final product fits the desired result, allow them to work at a pace and style that they are comfortable with. Nobody likes to be micromanaged, and if they do, they are probably too professionally immature to be working on a productive team. So, what exactly is micromanagement? How do we really define it? Micromanagement could be posited as taking great, wonderful, imaginative people, bringing them into your team, and then crushing their souls by telling them what font size to use. In the history of humankind, no one has ever told their team, *"We are not going to meet our goal if you use a Times New Roman font size 12!"*

If you were to take a moment and think about the times you have felt most tired in your job or the most stressed out you've ever been at work, it was probably when you had someone looking over your shoulder. While it is a good thing that you want to ensure things are running as smoothly as they should, micromanaging is counterproductive for all parties involved, especially for the employee you are trying to oversee. If you tell your employees exactly how they have to do something and check their work down to the smallest detail, they lose interest in their work and stop having fun.

Never tell people how to do things. Tell them what to do and they will surprise you with their ingenuity.
—General George Patton

Your employees are confronted with a flood of tasks that they need to get through. Sometimes, they need more time to work on a job, and that is understandable when you juggle multiple things at a time. That is why trust between a leader and their team is so important. A good leader measures performance based on the results of the work that is produced, not on how many hours your employee spends chained to their desk in a day.

Do you want another reason why micromanagement needs to stop? Because failure is not a bad thing, *setbacks should be thought of as a benefit*. Think about the past challenges and difficulties that you faced, which you managed to overcome eventually. Instead of looking at the downside, consider the takeaway lessons each setback left you with. Didn't it make you a much stronger person? Didn't it turn out to be a blessing in disguise? Didn't it add something of value to your life in a way you might not otherwise have had the opportunity of experiencing? If you give your team the chance to view each setback as a gift instead of a demotivating element, you will do wonders to transform their persistence and levels of motivation to do better. *Failure here becomes an achievement*, a main step upon the improvement of your team.

Not giving your employees at least some freedom to find their own way to get the result can be highly demotivating for them. Even worse, it might be so frustrating for them that they lose their desire to do any work at all, and their productivity levels drop. Once that happens, it is hard to ignite the spark that has died out.

Micromanaging your team is sending them a message that you don't trust them, and that you are not confident in their abilities to do what they were trained to do. If you are micromanaging your people, it needs to stop. It is okay that you want to control the results, and you need to do that because it is your responsibility to make sure work gets done. But it is *not okay* to specify and control every tiny little step towards the results! There is only one solution to micromanagement: *trust your team enough to set them free.*

Before we head to the conclusion, please let me know what you think about this book. I would really appreciate your review! Not only will it help me, but also everyone who is considering buying it. Just click the link below (or scan the QR code), and it will take you directly to the review page. Your feedback means a lot, thank you!

Amazon.com/review/create-review?&asin=Bo8HTXN46C

Conclusion

You will never feel truly satisfied by work until you are satisfied by life. —HEATHER SCHUCK

*I*ncredible accomplishments are possible when great teams work together in harmony. There is magic in different personalities coming together and working together to create a final result that everyone can be proud of. Great teamwork is the result of cooperation and the willingness to work together, embrace, and fit into other people's strengths and weaknesses. It is about commitment and the choice that is made every day to keep showing up for the people who are counting on you—the decision to continue being accountable for the needs of the collective, not just your own. Great teamwork is about contribution, about recognising that you may need to sacrifice some of your self-interests for the greater good at times. There is no *"I"* in the word team, and that means every member must be willing to give up the "me first" approach to reach the full height of what "we" can accomplish.

What it takes to become a great team is extraordinary but *entirely possible* at the helm of great leadership. There is no better feeling in the world than working alongside your team and coming out triumphant. To have worked hard, strived, fought, and sacrificed, and to accomplish something that could only be done because you worked together is a remarkable feeling. There is nothing quite like it. That is the beauty of teamwork and leadership, and that is how greatness is shaped.

As incredible as Michael Jordan's accomplishments are, he could not have done it on his own without the support of his team and coach (leader). Warren Buffet may have a brilliant mind, but his accomplishments are magnified because of the contributions and abilities of the people who work with him. This is the magic of collaboration. A truly inspiring leader can create a team that is able to look beyond the individual to focus on the collective and see the unbelievable talent of the unit as a whole. We know many successful people and the stories they have written, the legacy they have left behind. One of the reasons behind it all? *Teamwork*.

Finally, I encourage you to use the information from this book and put it into practice. Now, the ball is in your court to create a better work environment, leading to better teamwork and more success overall. Don't wait, start creating your own legacy right now!

PS: If you haven't already, don't forget to write a quick review right [here](). It only takes 60 seconds and would make me incredibly happy.

The Most Critical Core Values of a Successful Team

(Never lead a team without these 7 values.)

7 CORE VALUES OF A
SUCCESSFUL TEAM

Why is it important to set team values?

Values define what your company cares about. They represent the goals and intentions of an organisation, and tell employees how their work spirit should look like. If the wrong values are set, overall productivity and work relationships will get damaged.

To receive your Team Values List for **free**, visit this link:

https://starkingbooks.activehosted.com/f/1

Personal Notes

Personal Notes

Personal Notes

Personal Notes

Personal Notes

Personal Notes

Personal Notes

Personal Notes

Sources

6 Characteristics of a Bad Leader Everyone Hates! (2015, December 16). Retrieved from https://atmanco.com/blog/leadership/6-characteristics-of-a-bad-leader/

7 Organisation Stats You Need To Know. (2018, March 20). Retrieved from https://pickupplease.org/7-organization-stats/

8 Ways to Improve Diversity in the Workplace. (2016, November 28). Retrieved from https://hrdailyadvisor.blr.com/2016/11/28/8-ways-improve-diversity-workplace/

10 most ruthless leaders of all time. (2016, May 5). Retrieved from https://economictimes.indiatimes.com/people/10-most-ruthless-leaders-of-all-time/mao-zedong/slideshow/52120229.cms

28 Amazing Quotes That Will Inspire You to Get Organized. (2018, February 1). Order Your Life. https://orderyourlife.com/blogs/blog/28-amazing-quotes-that-will-inspire-you-to-get-organized

48 Funny and Inspirational Workplace Quotes. (2017, July 15). EmployeeConnect HRIS. https://www.employeeconnect.com/blog/funny-work-quotes-inspiration-workplace-quotes/

Ainomugisha, G. (2019, August 12). The Importance of Emotional Intelligence in Leadership. Retrieved from https://inside.6q.io/emotional-intelligence-in-leadership/

A quote from Tao Te Ching. (n.d.). Retrieved from https://www.goodreads.com/quotes/46410-a-leader-is-best-when-people-barely-know-he-exists

A quote from The Art of War. (n.d.). Retrieved from https://www.goodreads.com/quotes/811415-the-general-who-does-not-advance-to-seek-glory-or

Baer, D. (2016, June 14). How Only Being Able to Use Logic to Make Decisions Destroyed a Man's Life. Retrieved from https://www.thecut.com/2016/06/how-only-using-logic-destroyed-a-man.html

Benefits of Keeping Organised At Work. (n.d.). Retrieved from https://www.monster.ca/career-advice/article/benefits-of-keeping-organized-at-work

Bennett, A. (2016). *Case Study: The Great British Diversity Experiment.* Retrieved from https://www.sport.wales/files/b5392774eee97dccc5b0082a767417a2.pdf

Boyd, D. (2020, February 20). Workplace Stress. Retrieved from https://www.stress.org/workplace-stress

Chignell, B. (2019, July 31). Six reasons why fun in the office is the future of work. Retrieved from https://www.ciphr.com/advice/fun-in-the-office/

Christensen, K. (2020, November 16). 52 Best Work Life Balance Quotes To Inspire You | RealWealth.com. RealWealth. https://realwealth.com/work-life-balance-quotes/

Cortez, S. (2013, March 12). Anyone Who's Unemployed Should Spend At Least 20 Minutes Doing This Task. Retrieved from https://www.businessinsider.com.au/how-being-organized-affects-productivity-2012-6?r=US&IR=T

Emergenetics International. (2018, April 11). The Connection Between Vulnerability and Trust in Teams. Retrieved from https://www.emergenetics.com/blog/the-connection-between-vulnerability-and-trust-in-teams/

Emotional Intelligence in Leadership: Learning How to Be More Aware. (n.d.). Retrieved from https://www.mindtools.com/pages/article/newLDR_45.htm

Essentialism - The Disciplined Pursuit of Less by. (2019, April 23). Retrieved from https://gregmckeown.com/book/

Evans, B. D. (2020, February 6). Most CEOs Read A Book A Week. This Is How You Can Too (According To This Renowned Brain Coach). Retrieved from https://www.inc.com/brian-d-evans/most-ceos-read-a-book-a-week-this-is-how-you-can-too-according-to-this-renowned-.html

FORTUNE EDITORS. (2014, March 20). The World's 50 Greatest Leaders. Retrieved from https://fortune.com/2014/03/20/worlds-50-greatest-leaders/

Freiberg, K. A. J. (2019, April 7). 20 Reasons Why Herb Kelleher Was One Of The Most Beloved Leaders Of Our Time. Retrieved from https://www.forbes.com/sites/kevinandjackiefreiberg/2019/01/04/20-reasons-why-herb-kelleher-was-one-of-the-most-beloved-leaders-of-our-time/#57ce5869b311

G. (2019, June 3). Understanding the Differences: Leadership vs. Management. Retrieved from https://www.go2hr.ca/retention-engagement/understanding-the-differences-leadership-vs-management

Gallup 2019 Global Emotions Report - Gallup. (2020, April 8). Retrieved from https://www.gallup.com/analytics/248906/gallup-global-emotions-report-2019.aspx

Gleeson, B. (2016, November 9). 10 Unique Perspectives On What Makes A Great Leader. Retrieved from https://www.forbes.com/sites/brentgleeson/2016/11/09/10-unique-perspectives-on-what-makes-a-great-leader/#41ca1c165dd1

Hafezi, S. (2019, December 6). Are You Having Fun at Work? Retrieved from https://www.achievers.com/blog/are-you-having-fun-at-work/

Heath, V. (2019, July 29). Debate: Does diversity training work? Retrieved from https://www.gendereconomy.org/does-diversity-training-work/

Holmes, M. (2019, September 5). Why are there so few women CEOs? Retrieved from https://theconversation.com/why-are-there-so-few-women-ceos-103212

How to build trust at work. (n.d.). Retrieved from https://www.monster.com/career-advice/article/6-steps-to-building-trust-in-the-workplace-hot-jobs

Insight: What Dictators Have in Common. (n.d.). Retrieved from https://www.vision.org/insight-what-dictators-have-in-common-8859

J. (2021, February 18). The Best Emotional Intelligence Quotes of All Time. Sources of Insight. https://sourcesofinsight.com/emotional-intelligence-quotes/

Jenkins, R. (2020, February 6). The Underestimated Productivity Factor of Diversity and Inclusion. Retrieved from https://www.inc.com/ryan-jenkins/the-underestimated-productivity-factor-of-diversity-inclusion.html

Johnson, I. (2018, February 7). Who Killed More: Hitler, Stalin, or Mao? | Ian Johnson. Retrieved from https://www.nybooks.com/daily/2018/02/05/who-killed-more-hitler-stalin-or-mao/

Kottasova, I. (2014, December 1). Foreign name? Expect a tougher job hunt. Retrieved from https://money.cnn.com/2014/12/01/pf/jobs/foreign-names-jobs-discrimination/

Kruse, K. (2018, July 18). 100 Best Quotes On Leadership. Forbes. https://www.forbes.com/sites/kevinkruse/2012/10/16/quotes-on-leadership/?sh=30615cbf2feb

Landry, L. (2019, April 3). Emotional Intelligence in Leadership: Why It's Important. Retrieved from https://online.hbs.edu/blog/post/emotional-intelligence-in-leadership

Leadership Lessons from Cicero. (n.d.). Retrieved from https://www.luther.edu/ideas-creations-blog/?story_id=515847

Levy, C. P. (n.d.). Self-Discipline, a Must for Team Success | General Leadership. Retrieved from https://generalleadership.com/self-discipline/

M. (2020a, April 16). Improving Emotional Intelligence (EQ). Retrieved from https://www.helpguide.org/articles/mental-health/emotional-intelligence-eq.htm

MacKay, J. (2018, March 1). How to set smarter daily goals –. Retrieved September 4, 2020, from https://blog.rescuetime.com/daily-goals/#:%7E:text=Daily%20goals%20bring%20a%20level,I%20feel%20more%20in%20control

Metz, T. (2019, April 22). 5 Key Takeaways from Jeff Bezos' Leadership Style. Retrieved August 11, 2020, from https://pagely.com/blog/5-lessons-from-jeff-bezos-leadership-style/

Medrut, F. (2020, May 1). 25 Trust Quotes To Help You Build Stronger Relationships. Goalcast. https://www.goalcast.com/2020/05/01/trust-quotes/

Miller, C. C. (2018, April 24). The Top Jobs Where Women Are Outnumbered by Men Named John. Retrieved from https://www.nytimes.com/interactive/2018/04/24/upshot/women-and-men-named-john.html

Myatt, M. (2012, October 22). 15 Ways To Identify Bad Leaders. Retrieved from https://www.forbes.com/sites/mikemyatt/2012/10/18/15-ways-to-identify-bad-leaders/#25a908c715da

One third of your life is spent at work. (n.d.). Retrieved from https://www.gettysburg.edu/news/stories?id=79db7b34-630c-4f49-ad32-4ab9ea48e72b&pageTitle=1%2F3+of+your+life+is+spent+at+work

Orchestrating Impartiality: The Impact of "Blind" Auditions on Female Musicians | Gender Action Portal. (2020, March 1). Retrieved from https://gap.hks.harvard.edu/orchestrating-impartiality-impact-%E2%80%9Cblind%E2%80%9D-auditions-female-musicians

Peshawaria, R. (2012, July 28). There Is No Such Thing As Bad Leadership. Retrieved from https://www.forbes.com/sites/rajeevpeshawaria/2011/08/19/there-is-no-such-thing-as-bad-leadership/#6afa76d07b43

Play is an innate emotion in the brain, important to understanding autism, adhd, and child development. (n.d.). Retrieved from http://mybrainnotes.com/autism-adhd-play.html

Point/Counterpoint: Are Outstanding Leaders Born or Made? (2017, April 1). Retrieved from https://www.ncbi.nlm.nih.gov/pmc/articles/PMC5423074/

Powers, A. (2018, June 27). A Study Finds That Diverse Companies Produce 19% More Revenue. Retrieved from https://www.forbes.com/sites/annapowers/2018/06/27/a-study-finds-that-diverse-companies-produce-19-more-revenue/#49100807506f

Profile in Leadership: Amazon Founder Jeff Bezos. (n.d.). Retrieved August 11, 2020, from https://www.jacksonvilleu.com/blog/business/profile-in-leadership-amazon-founder-jeff-bezos/

Rampton, B. J. (2018, February 13). 7 Ways to Create Emotionally Intelligent Teams. Retrieved from https://execed.economist.com/blog/guest-post/7-ways-create-emotionally-intelligent-teams

Recruitment, C. (n.d.). 9 Ways to Promote Workplace Diversity in 2019 - Change Recruitment. Retrieved from https://www.changerecruitmentgroup.com/knowledge-centre/9-ways-to-promote-workplace-diversity-in-2019

Reynolds, K. (2019, July 10). 5 Strategies for Promoting Diversity in the Workplace. Retrieved from https://www.hult.edu/blog/promoting-diversity-in-workplace/

Ramos, T. (2018, November 27). Effective Leadership: Why It's Important And How It's Achieved. Retrieved from https://blog.runrun.it/en/effective-leadership/

Ryan, L. (2016, March 28). Management Vs. Leadership: Five Ways They Are Different. Retrieved from https://www.forbes.com/sites/lizryan/2016/03/27/management-vs-leadership-five-ways-they-are-different/#313a8bd269ee

Sexton, C. (2017, June 19). 7 Reasons Why Being Organized Boosts Productivity. Retrieved from https://theproductivityexperts.com/7-reasons-why-being-organized-boosts-productivity/

Strategic Leadership: The Essential Skills. (2019, March 12). Retrieved from
https://hbr.org/2013/01/strategic-leadership-the-esssential-skills
STRESS FACTS. (2018, December 12). Retrieved from
http://www.gostress.com/stress-facts/

Strauss, K. (2018, June 21). More Evidence That Company Diversity Leads To
Better Profits. Retrieved from
https://www.forbes.com/sites/karstenstrauss/2018/01/25/more-evidence-that-
company-diversity-leads-to-better-profits/#4a1ff8231bc7

Stress symptoms: Effects on your body and behavior. (2019, April 4). Retrieved
from https://www.mayoclinic.org/healthy-lifestyle/stress-management/in-
depth/stress-symptoms/art-20050987?reDate=18052020

T. (2018, May 2). 9 ways emotional intelligence improves team productivity.
Retrieved from https://medium.com/smells-like-team-spirit/group-eq-makes-
your-team-more-productive-at-work-we-have-proof-315eaa695190

Takala, T., & Auvinen, T. (2016, April 2). The Power of Leadership Storytelling:
Case of Adolf Hitler. Retrieved from
https://www.researchgate.net/publication/299599048_The_Power_of_Leaders
hip_Storytelling_Case_of_Adolf_Hitler

Team, C. (2019, October 23). How to Build Emotionally Intelligent, Productive
Teams. Retrieved from https://cmoe.com/blog/build-emotionally-intelligent-
productive-teams/

Team, T. (2020, March 18). The Importance of Discipline in Teamwork.
Retrieved from https://www.tbae.co.za/blog/the-importance-of-discipline-in-
teamwork/

Team, T. O. T. (2017, December 13). How to Have Fun at Work and Why it is Important. Retrieved from https://www.the1thing.com/blog/family-health-happiness/how-to-have-fun-at-work-and-why-it-is-important/

Team, V. C. C. (2021, March 18). 25 Powerful Diversity And Inclusion Quotes for a Stronger Company Culture. Nurture an Engaged and Satisfied Workforce | Vantage Circle HR Blog. https://blog.vantagecircle.com/diversity-and-inclusion-quotes/

Teamwork Blog | Product Updates, Customer Stories & Company News. (n.d.). Retrieved from https://www.teamwork.com/blog/

The Difference Between Leadership and Management. (n.d.). Retrieved from https://www.nextgeneration.ie/blog/2018/03/the-difference-between-leadership-and-management

The Leadership Lessons I Learnt From Niccolo Machiavelli. (2017, December 8). Retrieved from https://leaderonomics.com/leadership/leadership-lessons-machiavelli

Thiran, R. (2013, March 29). It Pays To Have Fun At Work! Retrieved from https://leaderonomics.com/leadership/it-pays-to-have-fun-at-work

Thomas, A. (2020, February 6). 15 Traits of the Worst Leaders (Avoid at All Costs). Retrieved from https://www.inc.com/andrew-thomas/15-traits-of-the-worst-leaders-avoid-at-all-costs.html

Three Differences Between Managers and Leaders. (2014, August 7). Retrieved from https://hbr.org/2013/08/tests-of-a-leadership-transiti

Tracy, B. (2019, August 13). 6 Time Management Skills For A Productive Life. Retrieved from https://www.briantracy.com/blog/time-management/6-time-management-tips-to-increase-productivity-organizational-skills/

What Are the Characteristics of a Good Leader? | CCL. (2020, April 27). Retrieved from https://www.ccl.org/blog/characteristics-good-leader/

What Is Emotional Intelligence, Daniel Goleman. (2020, April 15). Retrieved from https://www.ihhp.com/meaning-of-emotional-intelligence

Why diversity matters. (n.d.). Retrieved from https://www.mckinsey.com/business-functions/organization/our-insights/why-diversity-matters

Why Diversity Programs Fail. (2019, October 15). Retrieved from https://hbr.org/2016/07/why-diversity-programs-fail

Why Having Fun at Work is Important. (n.d.). Retrieved from https://www.kellyservices.us/us/careers/career-resource-center/managing-your-career/why-having-fun-at-work-is-important/

Workforce Diversity: A Key to Improve Productivity. (2014, January 1). Retrieved from https://www.sciencedirect.com/science/article/pii/S2212567114001786

Y. (2020, February 18). 15 Traits of a Terrible Leader. Retrieved from https://www.success.com/15-traits-of-a-terrible-leader/

Zitelmann, R. (2019, November 4). The Jack Ma Story: Why Thinking Big Is More Important Than Technical Knowledge. Retrieved August 11, 2020, from https://www.forbes.com/sites/rainerzitelmann/2019/11/04/the-jack-ma-story-why-thinking-big-is-more-important-than-technical-knowledge/#7ee32b70419c

Zojceska, A. (2020, April 3). How to Build, Manage and Promote Workplace Diversity? Retrieved from https://www.talentlyft.com/en/blog/article/246/how-to-build-manage-and-promote-workplace-diversity